Healthy Skin

Young Adult's Guide to the Science of Health

Healthy Skin

Rae Simons

CANE RIDGE

MASON CREST

Mason Crest
450 Parkway Drive, Suite D
Broomall, PA 19008
www.masoncrest.com

Printed in the Hashemite Kingdom of Jordan.

First printing
9 8 7 6 5 4 3 2 1

Series ISBN: 978-1-4222-2803-6
ISBN: 978-1-4222-2812-8
ebook ISBN: 978-1-4222-9008-8

The Library of Congress has cataloged the
       hardcopy format(s) as follows:

           Library of Congress Cataloging-in-Publication Data

Simons, Rae, 1957-
  Healthy skin / Rae Simons.
     pages cm. – (Young adult's guide to the science of health)
  Audience: Grade 7 to 8.
  Includes bibliographical references and index.
  ISBN 978-1-4222-2812-8 (hardcover) – ISBN 978-1-4222-2803-6 (series) – ISBN 978-1-4222-9008-8 (ebook)
  1. Skin–Care and hygiene–Juvenile literature. 2. Skin–Diseases–Juvenile literature. 3. Beauty, Personal–Juvenile literature. I. Title.
  RL87.S552 2014
  617.4'77–dc23
                  2013006388

Designed and produced by Vestal Creative Services.
www.vestalcreative.com

This book is meant to educate and should not be used as an alternative to appropriate medical care. Its creators have made every effort to ensure that the information presented is accurate and up to date—but this book is not intended to substitute for the help and services of trained medical professionals.

Contents

Introduction

by Dr. Sara Forman

You're not a little kid anymore. When you look in the mirror, you probably see a new person, someone who's taller, bigger, with a face that's starting to look more like an adult's than a child's. And the changes you're experiencing on the inside may be even more intense than the ones you see in the mirror. Your emotions are changing, your attitudes are changing, and even the way you think is changing. Your friends are probably more important to you than they used to be, and you no longer expect your parents to make all your decisions for you. You may be asking more questions and posing more challenges to the adults in your life. You might experiment with new identities—new ways of dressing, hairstyles, ways of talking—as you try to determine just who you really are. Your body is maturing sexually, giving you a whole new set of confusing and exciting feelings. Sorting out what is right and wrong for you may seem overwhelming.

Growth and development during adolescence is a multifaceted process involving every aspect of your being. It all happens so fast that it can be confusing and distressing. But this stage of your life is entirely normal. Every adult in your life made it through adolescence—and you will too.

But what exactly is adolescence? According to the American Heritage Dictionary, adolescence is "the period of physical and psychological development from the onset of puberty to adulthood." What does this really mean?

In essence, adolescence is the time in our lives when the needs of childhood give way to the responsibilities of adulthood. According to psychologist Erik Erikson, these years are a time of separation and individuation. In other words, you are separating from your parents, becoming an individual in your own right. These are the years when you begin to make decisions on your own. You are becoming more self-reliant and less dependent on family members.

When medical professionals look at what's happening physically—what they refer to as the biological model—they define the teen years as a period of hormonal transformation toward sexual maturity, as well as a time of peak growth, second only to the growth during the months of infancy. This physical transformation from childhood to adulthood takes place under the influence of society's norms and social pressures; at the same time your body is changing, the people around you are expecting new things from you. This is what makes adolescence such a unique and challenging time.

Being a teenager in North America today is exciting yet stressful. For those who work with teens, whether by parenting them, educating them, or providing services to them, adolescence can be challenging as well. Youth are struggling with many messages from society and the media about how they should behave and who they should be. "Am I normal?" and "How do I fit in?" are often questions with which teens wrestle. They are facing decisions about their health such as how to take care of their bodies, whether to use drugs and alcohol, or whether to have sex.

This series of books on adolescents' health issues provides teens, their parents, their teachers, and all those who work with them accurate information and the tools to keep them safe and healthy. The topics include information about:

- normal growth
- social pressures
- emotional issues
- specific diseases to which adolescents are prone
- stressors facing youth today
- sexuality

The series is a dynamic set of books, which can be shared by youth and the adults who care for them. By providing this information to educate in these areas, these books will help build a foundation for readers so they can begin to work on improving the health and well-being of youth today.

1

Your Skin

magine that it's morning and you just woke up. As you walk into the kitchen, you feel the soft brush of your cat's fur as she rubs against your bare ankles. You lean down to stroke her, and then you touch the coffeepot with your fingertips to see if it's hot. With a warm mug of coffee clasped between your hands, you wander outside; the wet grass is cold on your toes. You sink back into the hammock beneath the tree in your backyard, enjoying the cool air that presses against your face and bare arms, but a scratchy feeling on your leg disturbs your peace; a mosquito is biting you. With a sigh, you go back inside

the house and get ready for school. As you leave the house, your mother places a comforting hand on your back; her wordless touch lets you know how much she loves you. At the bus stop, a special person greets you and leans forward to press a kiss against your mouth. Your lips tingle, sending messages of pleasure and excitement to your entire body.

Thank Your Skin

You wouldn't have been able to experience any of the sensations we just described without your skin. Your skin allows you to feel softness and roughness … hot and cold … tickles and itches … pain and loving touches. Skin is an interface between the inside you and the outside world around you. It brings important messages to your brain, helping you to understand and interact with what-ever is going on.

Skin is made up of three layers—the epidermis, the dermis, and the subcutaneous layer. Each layer contains different structures that are important to your body's functioning.

The Epidermis

The epidermis is the outermost layer of your skin, the part you can see whenever you glance down at your hands or look into the mirror. This layer of cells that covers your body is elastic: it stretches when you move. If it didn't, you wouldn't be able to bend your knees and elbows—or smile and frown. And like a

Did you know that your hair and your nails are also a kind of modified skin?

strong rubber band, your skin quickly returns to normal when you straighten your arms or legs, or relax your facial muscles. Two types of fibers in your skin are what allow this to happen: collagen and elastin. Elastin is very stretchable, but collagen is strong and hard to stretch. Collagen is what keeps your skin from getting baggy and stretched out, and it works together with elastin to keep your skin smooth and flexible. As you grow older, though, you will have less and less collagen and elastin. This will cause wrinkles to form wherever your skin bends often.

When you look at your skin, you may think that nothing much is going on—but in fact, your epidermis is constantly hard at work. At the bottom of the epidermis, new skin cells are always forming. When they are ready, they move upward,

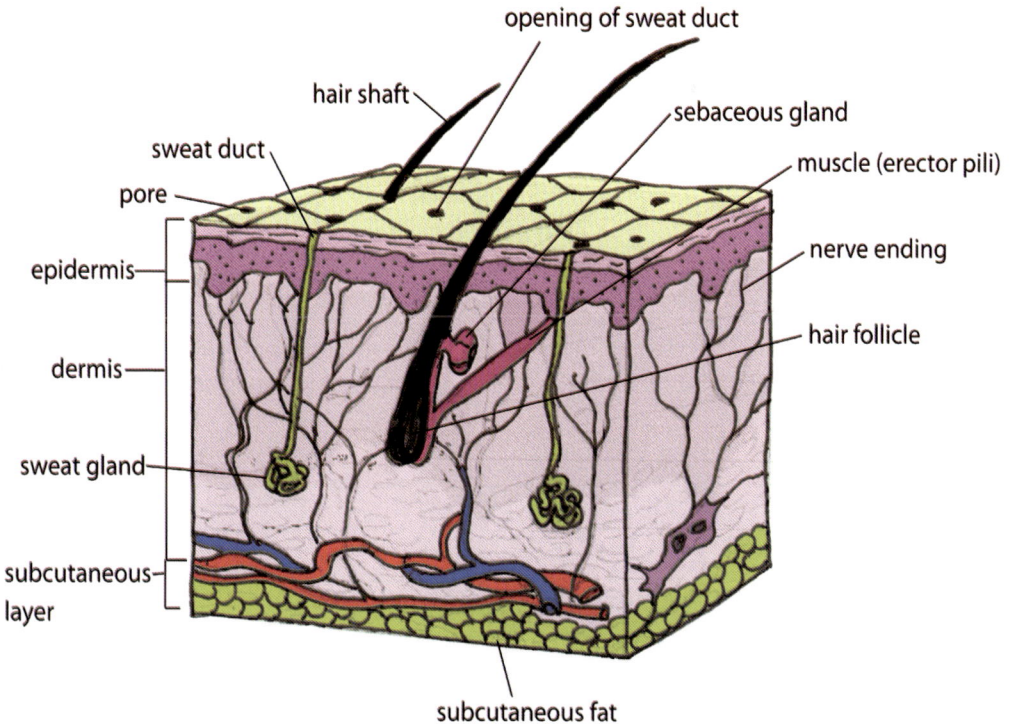

opening of sweat duct

hair shaft

sweat duct

pore

epidermis

dermis

sweat gland

subcutaneous layer

sebaceous gland

muscle (erector pili)

nerve ending

hair follicle

subcutaneous fat

Your Skin

toward the surface of the epidermis. Their journey takes them somewhere between two weeks and a month. Because the cells in your epidermis are completely replaced about every twenty-eight days, your skin will look smooth and youthful for many years, and any cuts and bruises you get will heal quickly.

As new cells form and move upward, their shape changes; they become flatter and spiny, then more GRANULOSE. In the up-

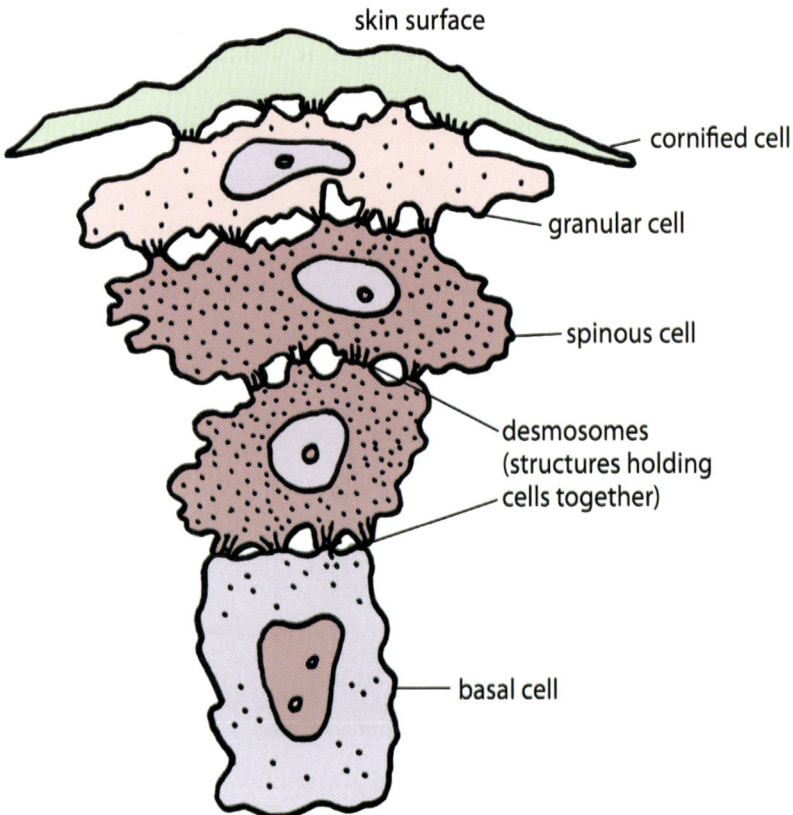

skin surface

cornified cell

granular cell

spinous cell

desmosomes
(structures holding
cells together)

basal cell

Healthy Skin

per layers, the granules discharge lipid, a special kind of fat that helps keep skin moist. These older cells look a little like a wall of bricks, with the lipids acting as the mortar between the cells.

Older cells that are closer to the top of your epidermis are constantly dying and being pushed up to the surface. So when you look at your skin, what you're really seeing is flattened, dead skin cells. But just because they are dead, doesn't mean these cells don't still have a job to do. They create a strong, durable layer that protects your body, a little like the bark on a tree. Eventually, though, the dead cells—which are also called corneocytes—flake off and are replaced by the next layer of cells.

On most parts of your body, your epidermis is only about as thick as a sheet of paper. Contained within this thin layer, though, are three different types of cells:

1. Melanocytes are the cells at the base of the epidermis that produce melanin; everybody has about the same number of melanocytes in their skin, but in dark-skinned people, these cells produce more melanin.
2. As skin cells move upward from the basal layer they start to produce a type of protein called karatin. (Your hair and nails are made up of a similar but harder substance.) The karatin-producing older cells are called karatinocytes.

Every minute of every day, you lose about 30,000 to 40,000 dead skin cells. Of course, each skin cell is very tiny, so it's not like you're going to leave a pile of dead skin cells on the floor every time you get up from your chair—but still, it adds up. Over the course of a year, you'll lose almost 10 pounds (4.5 kilograms) of dead cells!

3. Langerhans cells help protect your body against infection. These cells are spread through the keratinocytes. If any foreign substance—such as bacteria or pollution—finds its way through the skin's surface, the Langerhans cells whisk it away to be neutralized by special white blood cells in the LYMPH GLANDS.

Making new skin cells is the biggest job your epidermis does. Almost all the cells in your epidermis—as much as 95 percent of them—are continuously working to create new cells. The other five percent or so also have an important job. They create melanin.

Melanin is what gives your skin (and your hair) its color. The more melanin you have, the darker your skin will be. Melanin also helps shield your body from the sun's harmful ULTRAVIOLET rays (we'll find out more about this in chapter 5); when you spend time in the sun, your epidermis produces extra melanin to help protect you. That's why you get a suntan—or freckles.

The PIGMENT in melanin is made in tiny structures called melanosomes, which clump together like little grains of sand. The melanocytes deliver the melanosomes to the keratinocytes through slender FILAMENTS called dendrites; one melanocyte supplies about thirty-six keratinocytes with melanosomes. The tiny packages of pigment then cluster over the NUCLEUS of every cell that is exposed to sunlight.

Your eyelids have the thinnest skin of anywhere on your body—and your feet have the thickest. The soles of your feet have hundreds of layers of packed dead cells.

corneocytes

granular layer

spiny layer

basal layer

melanocyte

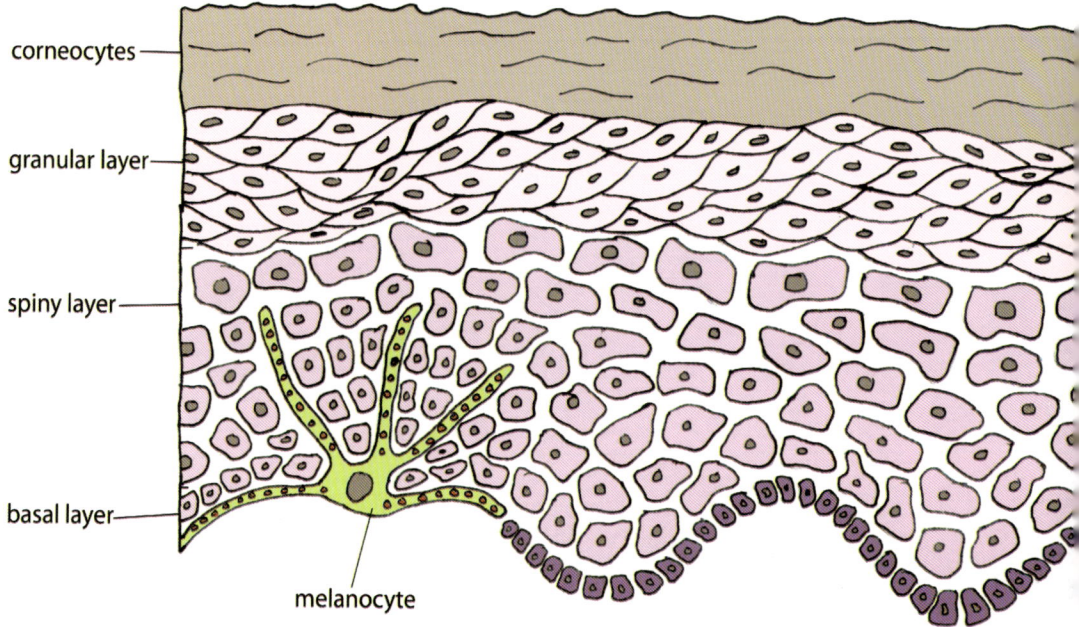

The melanin pigment comes in two forms. Eumelanin granules tend to be round and smooth; they produce black and brown skin colors. Phaeomelanin granules are more irregular in shape, and they produce red hair and freckles. Both forms of melanin, however, are often present together. The proportion of eumelanin you have compared to phaeomelanin will determine your skin and hair color.

The Dermis

The layer beneath the epidermis is called the dermis; it is connected to the epidermis by tiny projections called papillae. Although you can't see the dermis layer of your skin, it is still very important. The dermis is what contains nerve endings, tiny blood vessels, sweat glands, and sebaceous glands. Each of these structures has a role to play in keeping you and your skin healthy.

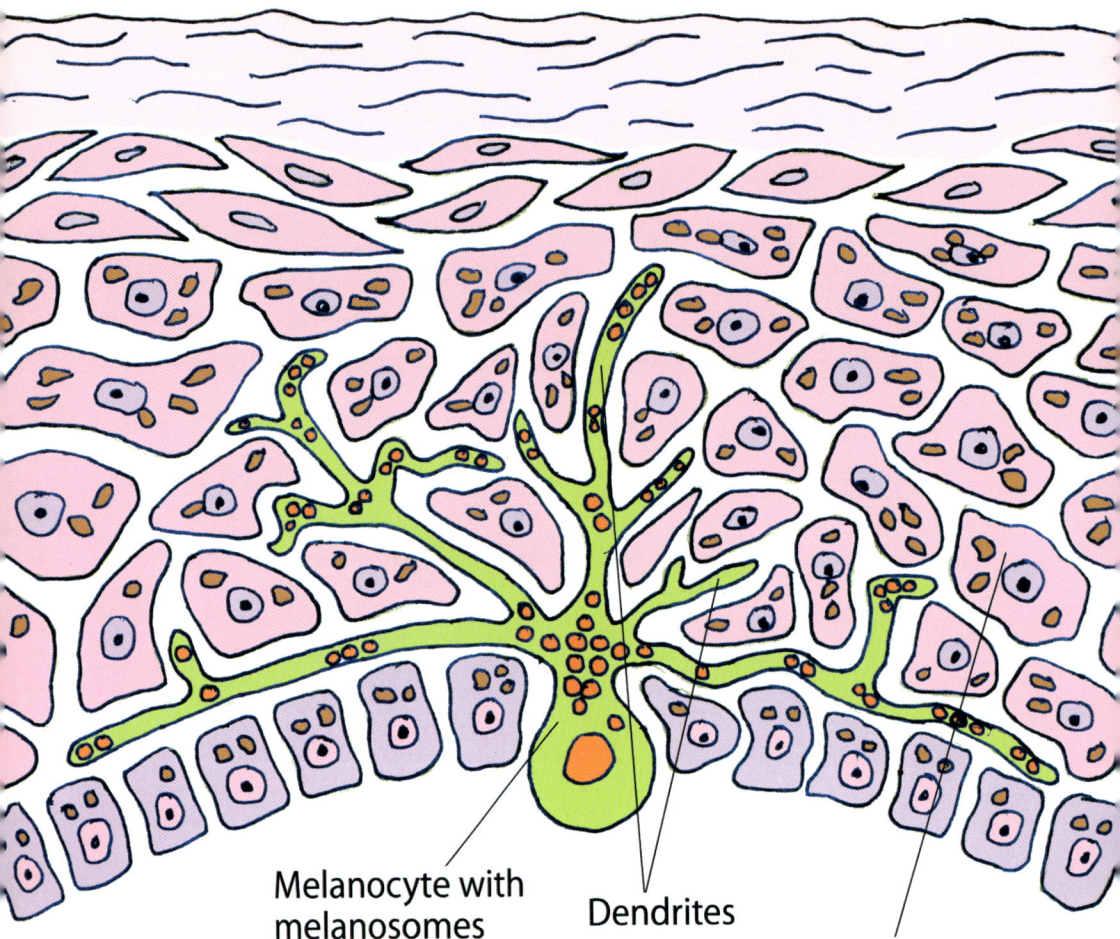

Melanocyte with melanosomes

Dendrites

Keratinocyte with melanin granules over the nucleus

Nerve Endings

Remember all those sensations you had during the imaginary morning we described at the beginning of this chapter? Each sensation you feel—heat and cold, soft and rough, wet and dry—is a message picked up from the outside world by the nerve endings in your dermis. These messages are then carried

Healthy Skin

to your brain, giving you important information about how you should act and react.

In some cases, the nerve endings in your dermis work with your muscles to protect your body from harm. For instance, say you picked up a hot potato. The nerve endings in the dermis of your fingertips would instantly send an "Ouch!" message to your brain or spinal cord—and the message is immediately sent back that tells your muscles to "Move!" This all happens far faster than we can describe, as fast or faster than a blink of your eye.

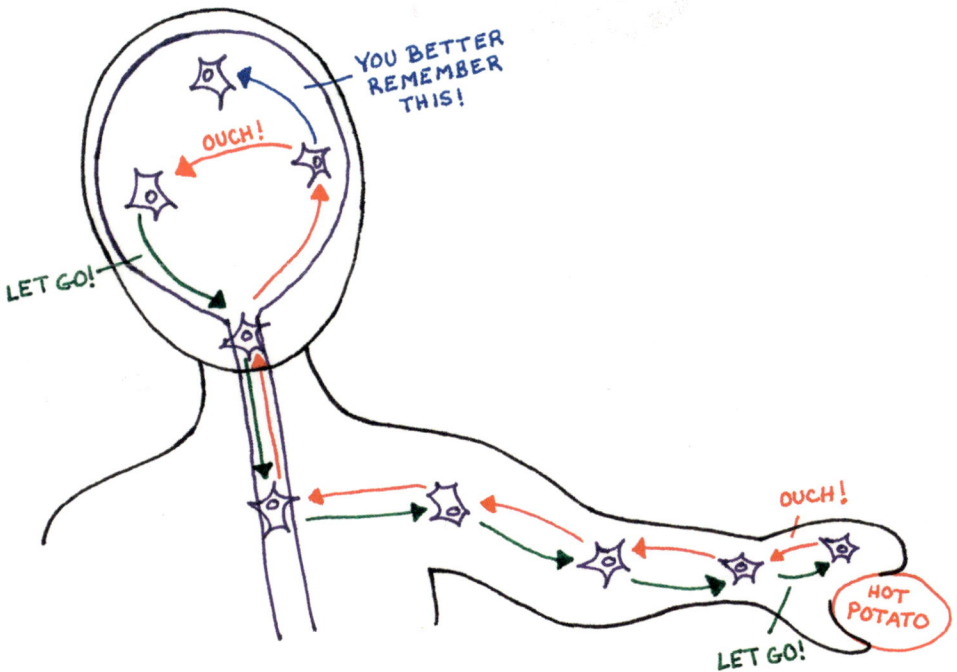

Your Skin

As people get older, their dermis gets thinner and their skin appears more transparent. That's why it's easier to see the blood vessels in older people's skin.

Blood vessels are your body's transportation system.

Healthy Skin

Even though you may not feel it, your body actually produces a tiny bit of sweat all the time. A normal healthy adult secretes about one pint of sweat every day. This amount is increased by physical activity.

Blood Vessels

The tiny blood vessels in your dermis bring oxygen and nutrients to your skin cells—and then they carry away wastes and carbon dioxide from the cells. This constant circulation helps keep your skin healthy—and the rest of you as well.

Sweat Glands

On a hot day, you'll soon find your skin becomes moist. That's because the body has a natural cooling system. Moisture is produced in your sweat glands in the dermis layer of your skin—and then it rises up to the epidermis through pores, tiny openings in your skin. The hotter your body becomes, the more sweat you will produce. As the sweat evaporates into the air, it helps to cool your entire body.

Unlike humans, many animals have few if any sweat glands, so their bodies have to find other ways to cool down. For instance, on a hot summer day a dog pants with his tongue hanging out, allowing the evaporation from his mouth's saliva to cool his entire body.

Soaking in the bathtub will temporarily remove the oil from your skin.

Apocrine glands are a special type of sweat glands that develop during PUBERTY and are concentrated in your armpits and PUBIC area. The sweat that comes from apocrine glands is thicker than the sweat produced other places on your body, and when it mixes with the bacteria on your skin's surface, it can become smelly. The apocrine glands are one reason why teenagers need to wash more often than they may have needed to when they were younger.

Sebaceous Glands

Sebum is your body's natural skin oil, and like sweat, it is produced by glands in the dermis. These are called sebaceous

Healthy Skin

glands, and they are constantly busy, creating the oil that keeps the outer layer of your skin lubricated and protected. Sebum also makes your skin waterproof. And when sebum and sweat mix together, they form a sticky, protective film over your skin's surface.

To see one way this film is useful to your everyday life, pick up a single piece of paper from the floor. You'll probably find you can do it quite easily—but now wash your hands well with soap and water, and then try again to pick up a piece of paper. You'll find it's not so easy this time, because your sticky layer of sebum and sweat has been washed away.

Something similar happens when you stay in the bathtub or a swimming pool for a long time. The water soaks off the sebum—and your skin becomes soggy. You may notice lots of white dead skin that didn't show up before. Before long, though, the sebaceous glands in your dermis will have produced a new protective film to cover your epidermis.

The oil from your sebaceous glands is also what gives your hair its shine. Connected to each hair follicle is a tiny sebaceous gland that releases sebum onto the hair. When each hair is lightly coated with oil, your hair shines. If you use harsh shampoos or soaps and wash away too much of this oil, your hair will become dry, rough, and brittle. And if you don't wash your hair enough, the sebum will build up, making your hair appear oily and stringy. Sebaceous glands can become overactive during puberty, which can lead to acne (see chapter 2) and oily hair that needs to be shampooed frequently. As you grow older, though,

The word subcutaneous comes from Latin roots: *sub*, which means "under, below," and *cutis*, which means "skin."

your sebaceous glands will not produce as much sebum, and you may have problems with dry skin and scalp.

The Subcutaneous Layer

The third and lowest layer of your skin is mostly made of fat. You may think that all fat is bad, but that is not the case; your subcutaneous fat plays an essential role within your body. It helps keeps you warm, and it also acts as the body's shock absorber, protecting the internal organs if you fall or bang into something. This subcutaneous layer helps to connect your skin to the tissues beneath it.

The subcutaneous layer is also where your hair has its roots, the base of the tiny tubes called hair follicles. The follicles begin in the subcutaneous layer and travel up through the dermis. You have hair follicles all over your body, except for the palms of your hands, the soles of your feet, and your lips.

Skin and Body Temperature

When you go outside on a chilly day, your body temperature doesn't fall to match the temperature of the air around you. And if you play a fast game of tennis in the summer, your temperature won't normally soar to dangerous heights. That's because the various parts of your skin play an important role in keeping your body temperature right around 98.6 degrees Fahrenheit (37 degrees Celsius).

The HYPOTHALAMUS is the body's inner thermostat. It sends messages to the skin that keep the body's temperature regulated. So when you exercise on a hot day, the hypothalamus

Healthy Skin

sends a message to release some of the body's heat. The blood vessels in your skin do this by bringing warm blood closer to the surface where it can cool off. (That's why you may look flushed and red after you've been exercising.) Your sweat glands will also do their part to cool the body down.

When your body is exposed to cold, the hypothalamus also swings into action. It sends another message to the blood vessels in your skin, this time causing them to become as narrow as possible, keeping the warm blood away from the surface. Your pilomotor reflex will also kick in, causing tiny muscles—called arrector pili muscles—to pull on your hairs so that they stand up very straight. In other words, you get goosebumps.

The hair on your head helps keep you warm all the time by preventing heat from escaping from the top of your head; it

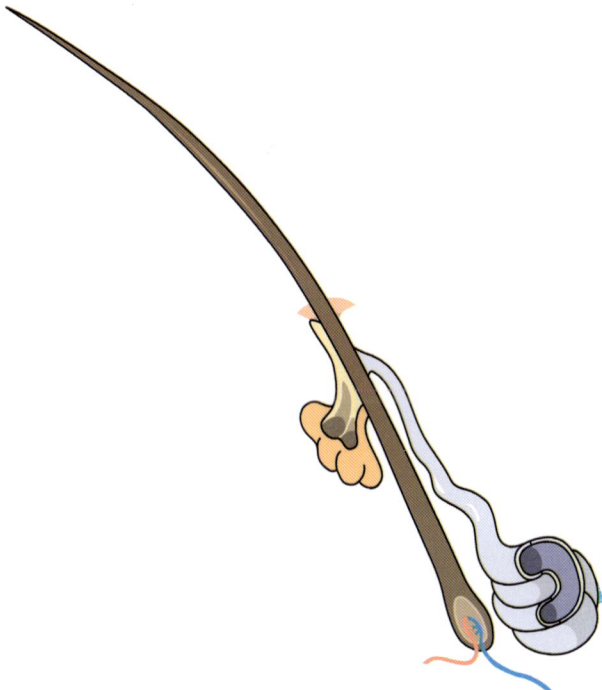

Sebaceous glands and sweat glands are located next to the hair follicles.

Your skin is your body's largest organ. If we could stretch out the skin of an average 150-pound adult so that it lay flat, it would cover approximately two square yards—about the size of a shower curtain—and it would weigh about nine pounds.

Healthy Skin

also cushions your head against injury. Hair serves other important functions as well. For example, the hair inside your nose and ears and around your eyes protects you from dust and other foreign particles.

The Organ Everyone Sees

Your skin protects the network of muscles and blood vessels, nerves, and tissues that cover your bones. It forms a barrier that keeps harmful substances and germs from entering the body. It guards your delicate internal organs against injury, and it keeps you from losing important fluids that bring life to body tissues.

But don't assume that your skin is just your outer layer, a sort of envelope, with no real function other than to contain your insides. In reality, your skin is an organ, just like your heart and your lungs and your kidneys—except no one can see those other organs. You probably don't really care what your heart or your liver looks like, but chances are you do care how your skin looks. After all, it's the one body organ that everyone can see.

Your skin is very important to your appearance, and as a result it may play a vital role in your self-concept. Someone who has healthy, glowing skin may feel better about himself than another person who has some kind of skin condition. It's hard to disguise a skin disorder. Unless you hide under a giant paper bag, your skin is right out there where everyone can see. If you have a skin condition like acne or eczema or some of the other disorders we'll discuss in the chapters that follow, you may feel as though your skin is a nuisance you wish would disappear.

But you couldn't live without your skin. Not only would you look pretty strange with all your naked blood and muscles showing, but your skin performs important functions that are essential to your entire health.

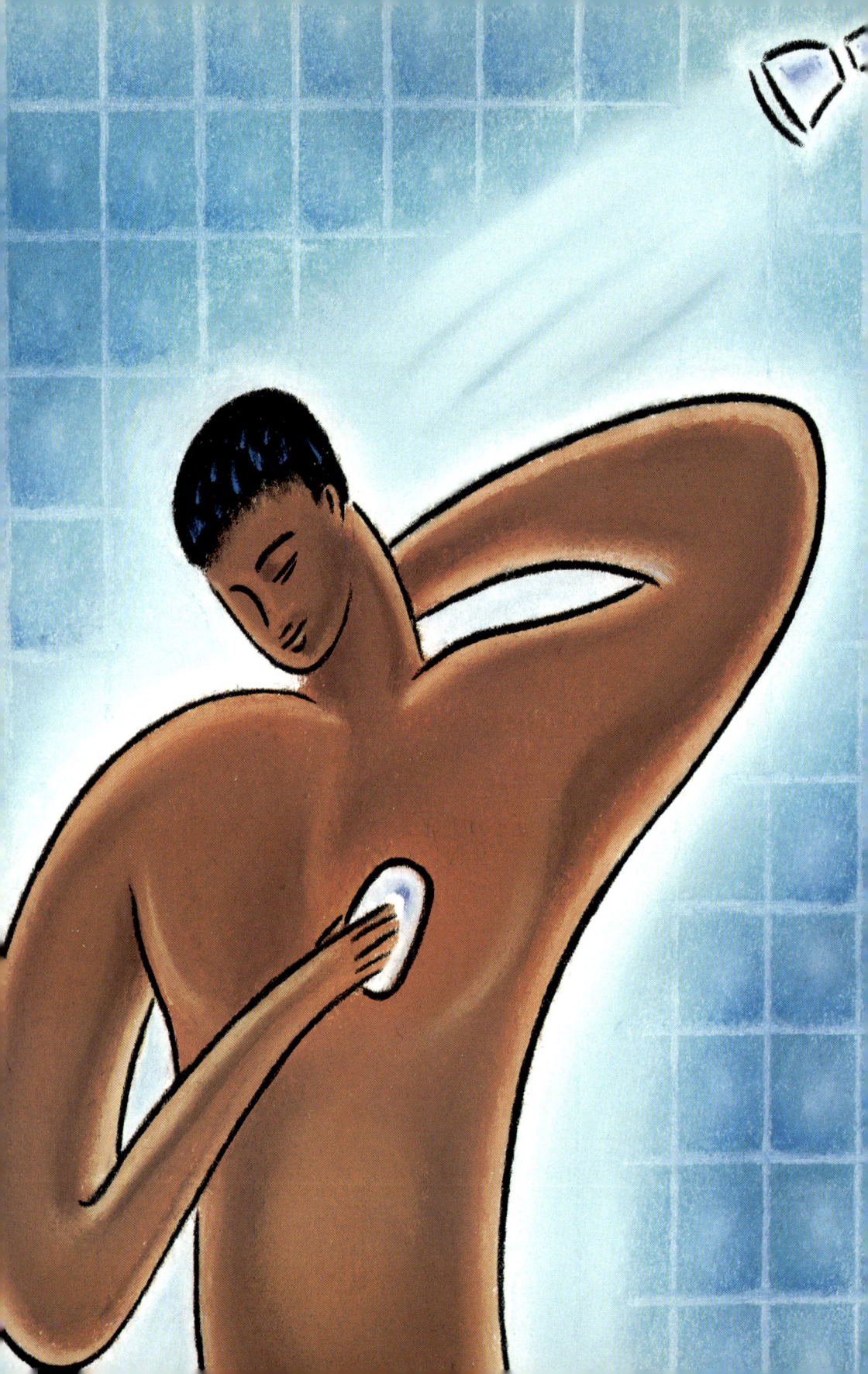

2

Acne

Imagine again that you've just woken up one morning—but this time, you instantly remember that today is a big day. Maybe it's the day of the prom, or maybe you'll be giving a speech in front of your entire class, or you have an interview for your first job. But wouldn't you know it: you feel a suspicious throbbing tingle on your face. When you look in the mirror, your fears are confirmed: an enormous, red pimple has erupted on your skin.

Unfortunately, acne is a part of growing up. Pimples form when the pores in your skin become clogged with sebum, the oily substance that lubricates your skin and hair. During puberty, your HORMONES go into overdrive, sending out the mes-

Mild acne includes the whiteheads and blackheads that almost everyone gets at one time or another. These are caused by pores becoming clogged with dirt and oil.

sage to your skin to produce lots of sebum, more than you need. Many sebaceous glands are found on the forehead, nose, and chin, as well as your back—so these areas are where you are most apt to get pimples.

Preventing Acne

You've probably heard lots of ways to fight acne. Some of these methods may be good practices to follow—but there are a lot of myths about acne as well. Here are some examples you may have heard:

MYTH: Chocolate and greasy foods cause acne.
FACT: Eating too many sweets and high-fat foods is not good for you; these are high-calorie foods that can make you overweight, while offering you little in the way of nutrition. But researchers have proven that acne is not caused by what you eat.

MYTH: Squeezing your pimples will help them heal more quickly.
FACT: Although it's tempting to pop that nasty zit that's appeared on your face, whenever you squeeze a pimple, you push bacteria into the skin, causing more swelling and redness. The pimple may temporarily look smaller, but it will stay around longer. Squeezing it may also cause a red or brown mark or a scar to form. These discolorations can last for months before they

fade away, and without special medical intervention, dents and pits in your skin will last forever.

MYTH: If you get a suntan, your pimples will go away.
FACT: Your pimples may not be as noticeable if you're tanned—but the sun can dry out your skin and irritate it, making it more susceptible to future acne. Research has found no link whatsoever between exposure to the sun and pimples. The sun's rays can have harmful effects, though, as we'll discuss in chapter 5.

MYTH: The more you wash your face, the fewer pimples you will have.
FACT: Staying clean is a vital part of preventing acne breakouts, since soap and water help remove dirt and oil from your pores. But washing your face too often or scrubbing it too hard can ir-

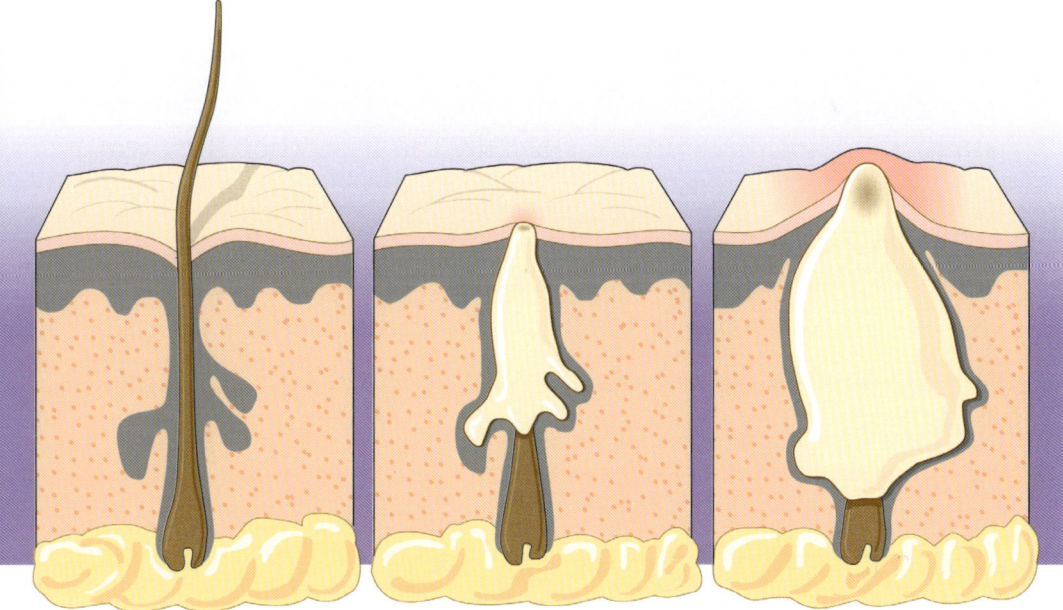

A pimple forms when a pore becomes clogged with sebum.

Acne

ritate your skin—and skin that is raw and sore is vulnerable to the bacteria that helps cause pimples.

MYTH: The more acne medication you use, the fewer pimples you will have.
FACT: Most over-the-counter acne medications contain drying agents like benzoyl peroxide and salicylic acid. These substances can keep your skin from producing too much sebum—but too much of these chemicals can make your skin too dry. The same as too much sun or too much washing, too much acne medication can irritate your skin and make it more susceptible to bacteria. (If you're taking a prescription medication for acne, always be sure to follow your doctor's directions exactly, even if the medicine doesn't seem to be working at first. Many acne medications take as long as eight weeks to make a noticeable difference.)

MYTH: Makeup causes pimples.
FACT: It's true that some cosmetics can irritate your skin, and heavy powders and creams may help clog your pores. However, many kinds of makeup are specially made so that they won't cause acne breakouts. Look for cosmetics that say they are "non-acnegenic" or "noncomedogenic." Some concealers even contain benzoyl peroxide or salicylic acid, which help fight pimples. If you notice that a particular kind of makeup irritates your skin, however, always stop using it. And if you have moderate to se-

Moderately severe acne is the term used for clogged pores that have become red and swollen. These are called papules. When the pimple has a white center, it is called a pustule.

vere acne, you may want to talk to a doctor about which cosmetics are best for you.

There's not much teens can do to avoid pimples altogether; they're a part of almost every teenager's life. But there is plenty you can do to help control acne breakouts. Here are a few tips:

- Wash your face twice a day with warm water and a cleanser formulated specially for people with acne. Be careful not to scrub your face so hard that you irritate your skin.
- Once or twice a day, use an over-the-counter lotion containing benzoyl peroxide (recommended by the American Academy of Dermatology).
- Try to avoid touching your face with your fingers; if you use makeup, always wash your hands before applying it to your skin. Making these practices a habit will help keep bacteria away from your skin's vulnerable pores.
- Wash your pillowcases, sheets, and blankets often so that dirt, dead skin, and skin oil won't build up on them and be transferred to your face.
- If you wear glasses or sunglasses, clean them often to help prevent skin oil from clogging your pores where your glasses touch the skin around your eyes and nose.
- Drink lots of water. Water helps keep your skin healthy, and it aids in flushing dirt from your pores.
- If you wear makeup, wash it off before you go to bed. Throw away any old makeup that smells or looks different from when you bought it.
- If you get acne on your back or other parts of your body, try to wear soft, loose, natural fabrics that will absorb sweat, prevent irritation, and allow your skin to breathe.

Avoid wearing scarves, headbands, or caps, as these can collect dirt and oil.

· Keep your hair clean and out of your face, since your pores may become clogged from the additional sebum on your hair.

Most teens who make these tips a part of their everyday routines are able to take control of their acne. Some people, however, have more severe breakouts. If you carefully follow all these suggestions, and you're still getting lots of pimples, you may want to talk to a dermatologist. And if you have nodules, the hard, painful lumps that are larger than ordinary pimples, you should see your doctor or DERMATOLOGIST right away. He will be able to help you find the treatment method that's best for you.

Most likely, your doctor will prescribe some combination of TOPICAL creams or gels. If your acne is severe, she may also prescribe ANTIBIOTICS or some other oral medication, such as isotretinoin. ORAL CONTRACEPTIVES can sometimes help teenage girls with acne by helping to control the hormones that some-times trigger skin problems.

Coping with Acne Scars

Maybe you've started taking care of your skin as carefully as you can—but you already have scars from the pimples you used to get, and those scars aren't going away. Or maybe you're doing ev-

Severe acne is the term used for painful, pus-filled lumps (called nodules) that form under the skin.

Healthy Skin

Acne

erything right, but your pimples still leave scars. If you have the painful nodules caused by severe acne, you are especially apt to get scars. What can you do?

If you have reddish or brownish marks left by pimples, they will eventually fade by themselves. They may take as long as a year to go away, though, so you'll have to live with them in the meantime. If you use makeup, you can hide the marks with a concealer cream—but don't load it on so heavily that you clog your pores still more.

True scars are caused either by loss of skin tissue—or by extra tissue formation. The scars caused by loss of tissue are the most common. They are similar to the scars caused by chickenpox, and they may leave small "ice-pick" marks on your face. The scars caused by increased tissue formation are called keloids or hypertrophic scars. This type of scar is caused by the overproduction of collagen (see chapter 1) in response to an injury. The collagen becomes piled up in a fibrous mass, which causes a smooth scar that can be as large as an inch (more than a centimeter). These scars last for years, but they may get smaller with time.

If you consult a doctor about either of these kinds of scars, he may suggest a chemical peel. This procedure can be done in his office, and it helps improve the appearance of your skin by removing the rough upper layer of dead skin cells.

For more serious scarring, your doctor may recommend some form of dermatologic surgery. This is a decision you will

Healthy Skin

need to talk over with your doctor and your parents. There are many things you will need to consider:

- What can your family afford? Some kinds of treatments are more expensive than others. Does your family have medical insurance that will cover these kinds of expenses?
- How do you feel about your scars? Do you feel they are affecting you socially and emotionally—or are you willing to live with them?
- How severe are your scars? You may think that they're so awful that no one can keep from staring at you—but they may in fact not be as noticeable as you think. Your friends and family may be able to help you reach a more objective view of your scars.
- How much time are you willing to spend pursuing treatment? Some treatment methods take time, and many will need to be repeated again after a few months or a year.
- How will your skin respond to various forms of treatment? If you are very susceptible to scarring, some kinds of treatment might actually result in more scars. A dermatologist will be able to assess what will work best for your skin.

Your parents and doctor can help you find the answers to these questions. But ultimately, only you can decide how much your scars bother you and what you are willing to endure to correct them.

Kinds of Scar Treatment

If you decide to pursue scar treatment, you will be faced with several options.

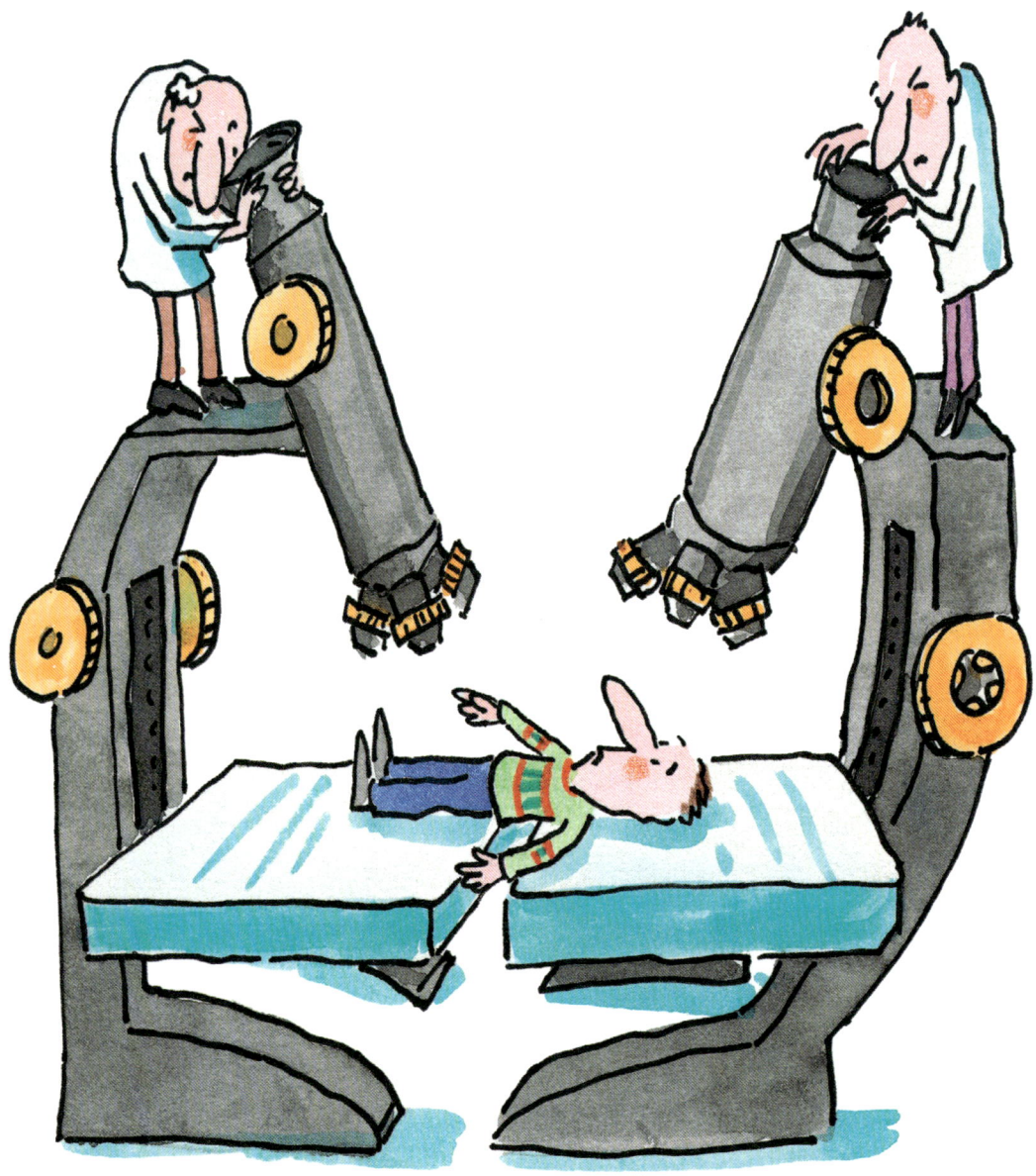

Healthy Skin

After dermabrasion, skin usually takes between one and three weeks to heal. Your skin may appear red for several months.

Collagen Injection

Collagen from cows, other animals, or human beings is injected under the skin to fill in certain types of scars. This is not usually a permanent solution, since the benefits of collagen injection generally last for only three to six months. Additional collagen injections can be performed—but this can get expensive.

Dermabrasion

This method is often considered by dermatologists to be the most effective treatment for acne scars. If you were to opt for this treatment, you would receive a LOCAL ANESTHETIC, and then a high-speed spinning wire brush or diamond instrument would remove the surface skin from your face or other affected areas. As the skin heals, a new, smoother layer of skin replaces the scarred skin. Superficial scars may be removed altogether by this method, and deeper scars may be less noticeable.

However, this method is not good for everyone. If you have "ice-pick scars," they may actually become more noticeable after dermabrasion, since the scars are wider under the skin than they are at the surface. And if you have dark skin, dermabrasion may cause changes in your coloring.

Laser Treatment

This is one of the newest forms of scar treatment. Like dermabrasion, this method removes the damaged top layer of your

skin—but instead of using a brush or other instrument, lasers are used to remove the upper tissue and tighten the middle layer of skin, leaving it smoother. The doctor will first numb your skin with a local anesthesia, and the treatment will then last anywhere from a few minutes to an hour. Afterward, your skin will heal in only three to ten days; because your tissue absorbs the laser's powerful energy, however, your skin may be red for several months.

Fat Grafting

This treatment method takes fat from your own body and injects it beneath the surface of your skin in order to fill in hollowed-out scars. This method is most often used to correct the deep scars left by severe acne's nodules. Over six to eighteen months, however, your body will reabsorb the fat, so the procedure will usually need to be repeated. Later treaments may last longer than the first procedure did, but they will still probably need to be repeated at least once.

Skin Surgery

During this procedure, the scar is cut down to the deepest layer of your skin, the subcutaneous fat. The skin is then repaired with tiny SUTURES. In some cases, a surgical probe is

used to lift the scarred tissue away from the unscarred skin, allowing a hollowed out scar to be elevated.

Skin Grafting

In some cases, dermabrasion or laser treatments may uncover a network of tunnels beneath the skin's surface. These tunnels are created when the sebaceous glands become inflamed and infected. Skin grafts (attaching a piece of skin from elsewhere on your body) to your face may be necessary to close up these tunnels.

Keloid Treatment

Keloids are the type of scar that is the most difficult to treat. If your skin has a tendency to form keloids in response to acne, then it will also tend to form keloids in response to any kind of surgical intervention. Sometimes, though, STEROIDS are injected into the skin around the keloid scar, or topical retinoic acid may be applied directly to the scar. Other methods of treating keloid scars include radiation or surgery.

The Social and Emotional Effects of Acne

Back when your grandparents were teenagers and young adults, medical researchers were already aware of the impact ordinary pimples can have on the emotional and social lives of teenagers. Researchers Sulzberger and Zaldems wrote in 1948:

There is no single disease which causes more psychic trauma, more maladjustment between parents and children, more general insecurity and feelings of inferiority and greater sums of psychic suffering than does acne.

And yet most adults who no longer get pimples take acne for granted as an expected part of the teenage years. After all, everyone gets pimples—and no one dies from them. Eventually, even the worst zits go away by themselves.

Recent psychological studies, however, have found that the effects of acne can be more serious than many people may have expected. The following emotions and characteristics were common among people with moderate to severe acne:

- social withdrawal
- poor self-esteem
- negative body image
- diminished self-confidence
- embarrassment
- depression
- frustration
- anger
- preoccupation; difficulty focusing on the outside world around them
- higher rates of unemployment among adults

"It is really humiliating to feel like I have no control over my acne. I hold my head down and I am ashamed to look at people."

Quote from a person with acne; www.skincarephysicians.com/acnenet/socimpct.html

These feelings and characteristics are almost always interrelated with each other; the effect of one leads to another, which in turn only makes the other effects still worse. For example, if you lack self-confidence, you're apt to withdraw socially, and this in turn will tend to make you depressed, and your self-esteem will suffer. It's like a snowball that just gets bigger and bigger the more it rolls down the hill. And to think something as seemingly small as a pimple was what started the snowball rolling!

Don't let acne take control of your life. Create the habits you'll need to deal with this skin condition—and if you need help from a doctor, don't be afraid to ask.

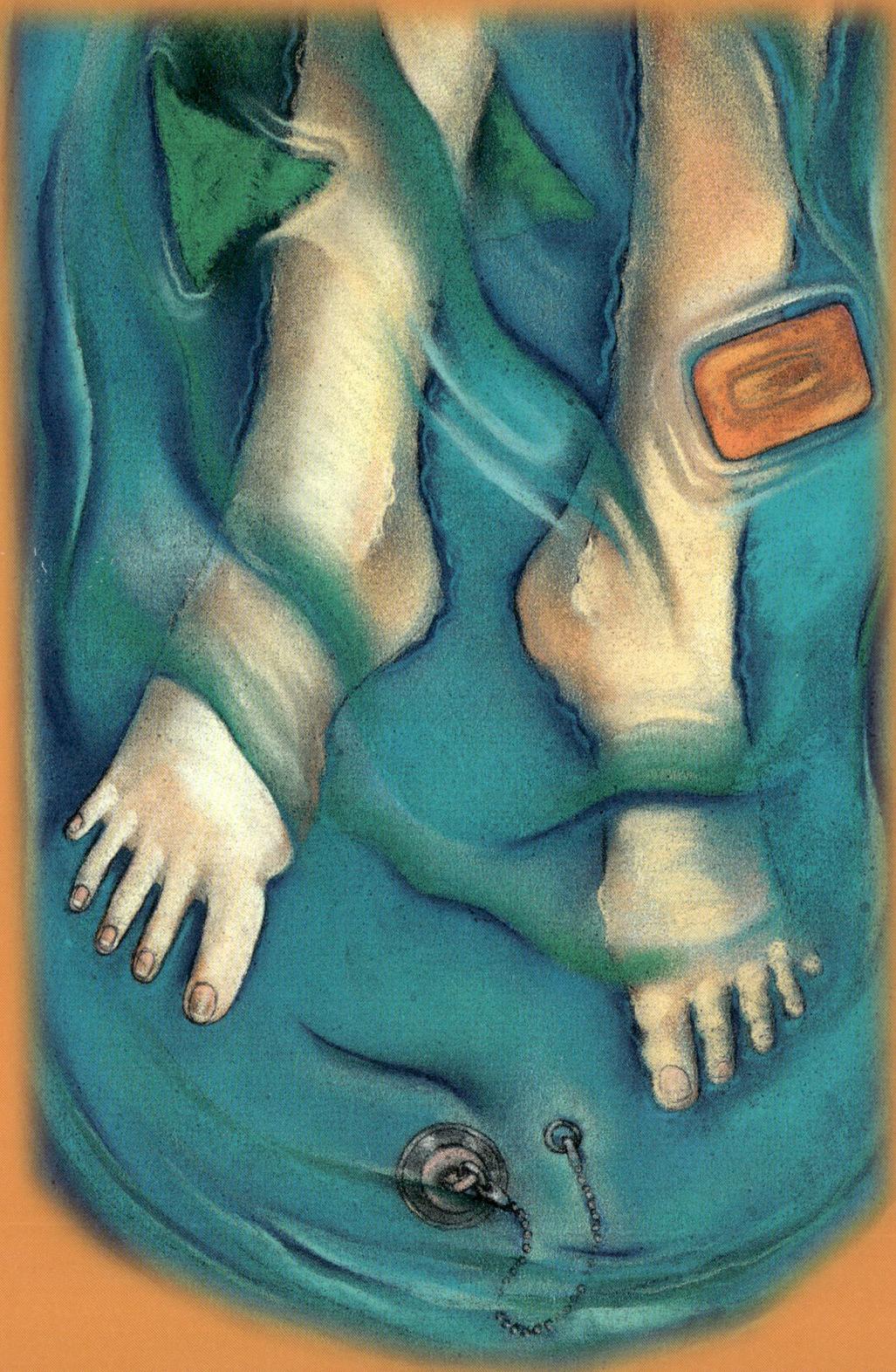

3

Itchy Rashes and the Various Skin Disorders That Cause Them

Ryan woke up itching. Earlier that evening, he and his friends had cooked hotdogs on a fire in Ryan's backyard. A few mosquitos had whined around their heads—but the itch on Ryan's ankles and hands felt worse than any mosquito bite he'd ever had. He couldn't seem to keep his fingers from scratching, even though it just made his skin burn and itch that much more. Finally, he got up and stumbled to the bathroom.

In the light, he could see that his feet, ankles, arms, and hands were covered with a red, watery rash. He yanked the medicine cabinet open, looking for anything that might help him.

"What did you get into?" asked his mother from the door into the hallway. She took a step closer and looked at his hands and feet. "Oh no. Were you poking around in the weeds under the trees? Didn't you hear me warning you boys not to go back there?"

Ryan shrugged. "I guess I wasn't paying attention. I went to look for more wood for the fire."

"And you were barefoot, weren't you? And then you picked up the wood and carried it back in your arms. Did you happen to notice a sort of vine growing on the wood?"

"I guess maybe." Ryan looked down at his itchy hands. "What is it?"

His mother gave him a rueful smile. "Poison ivy. The good news is you won't die. The bad news is you're going to be pretty miserable for a while."

The rash from poison ivy is just one form of dermatitis, a skin inflammation. When the skin comes in contact with an irritating substance—like poison ivy—it becomes inflamed and causes contact dermatitis. This painful, itchy condition can be

Healthy Skin

caused by many other substances, including the chemicals in laundry soap, makeup, and perfume. Sometimes metals like nickel found in inexpensive jewelry can also cause contact dermatitis.

Dermatitis is just one kind of skin disorder; other skin conditions are caused by bacteria, fungi, viruses, or parasites. Ringworm, for example, is caused by a fungus that makes scaly, ring-shaped LESIONS on the skin. (Despite its name, ringworm is not caused by a worm.) Athlete's foot and yeast infections are also caused by fungal infections, while viral infections produce the rashes that go along with chicken pox, measles, and other illnesses. Parasites like SCABIES and lice can also cause an itchy rash.

Poison ivy leaves.

Itchy Rashes

Eczema

Sara thought she might go crazy if she didn't stop itching. The backs of her knees, her chest and neck, and worst of all, patches on her face were all covered with red blisters that felt hot and itchy. She had scratched her wrists and inside the folds of her

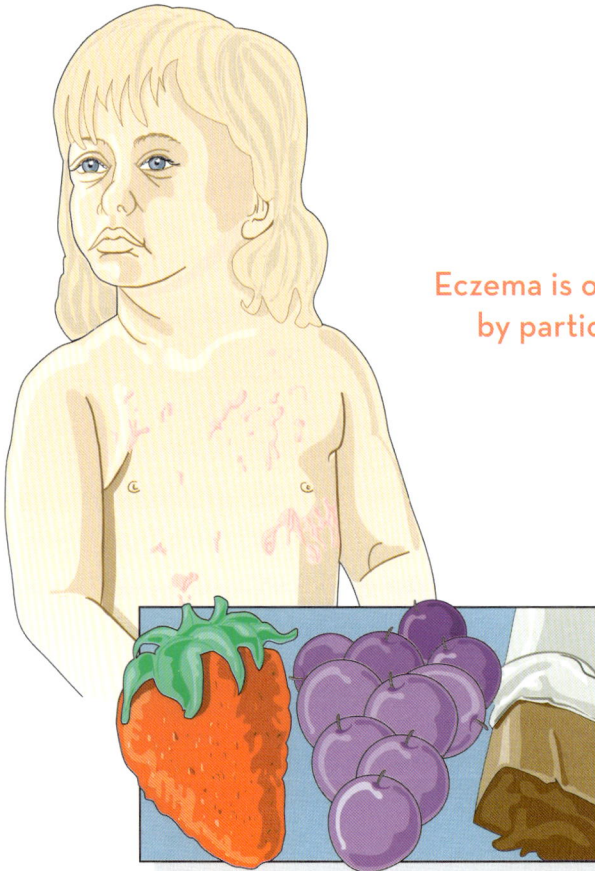

Eczema is often triggered by particular foods.

Candidal dermatitis—yeast infections—form in warm, moist environments. The folds of skin in a baby's diaper area are susceptible to this skin disorder, but candidal dermatitis is also a common vaginal infection among teen girls. Over-the-counter creams can clear up this annoying and itchy condition, or a doctor can prescribe an oral medication.

elbows so much that her skin there felt like leather. Her parents were always pestering her not to scratch, and Sara had to admit that the more she scratched, the worse she felt—but she couldn't seem to help herself. When her mother decided to take Sara to a doctor, Sara was relieved. Maybe the doctor would be able to tell her what was wrong. Even better, maybe he would make her terrible itching go away.

Sara has eczema, a group of skin conditions that cause the skin to become easily irritated; the most common is atopic eczema. It can occur at any age, but it is most common in babies, children, and young adults. Doctors aren't exactly sure what causes atopic eczema, but they suspect that people like Sara who have this condition also have an IMMUNE SYSTEM that reacts to the environment differently than most people's.

If you don't have eczema, but you know someone like Sara who does, don't worry—eczema isn't contagious. Most teens who have this condition, however, have a family member who has it as well, so researchers suspect that eczema is often (but not always) passed on through the GENES.

Allergies may play a role in this itchy skin disorder. Some of the teens who have eczema also have asthma and hay fever. For about 30 percent of the people who have eczema, allergies to

various foods (for example, milk, eggs, fish, wheat, or strawberries) may bring on a rash or make an existing condition even worse. Allergies to animal DANDER, rough fabrics, and dust may also trigger eczema.

If you have eczema, you should do your best to avoid anything you know causes your condition to get worse. Sometimes, though, it's simply impossible to avoid everything that makes

A new facial soap can sometimes trigger contact dermatitis.

you itch. Like Sara, you may feel frustrated and desperate from itching so much—and embarrassed by the inflamed skin that covers parts of your body.

That's why it's a good idea to consult a medical practitioner if you think you may have eczema. Your doctor will want to first rule out contact dermatitis (a rash that's caused by your skin being irritated by one particular substance, like a detergent or a piece of jewelry). Since diagnosing atopic eczema can be difficult, your doctor may want to refer you to a specialist, a dermatologist.

Your doctor or dermatologist will probably want to review your medical history. This means she will ask you lots of questions about your past health, as well as the health of your family members. She will want to know if you've recently started using a new lotion or soap, or if your family has switched laundry detergents. She may also ask you about what's going on in your life, to determine if you've been under emotional stress.

Once your doctor has decided you have eczema, he will help you determine which activities and environmental triggers are making your rashes worse. He may also prescribe a topical cream that contains a corticosteroid, a substance that helps soothe your itch. Other medications that you take internally—like antihistamines or corticosteroids—may also help control the itching. If you have severe eczema, your doctor may use ultraviolet light therapy to help clear up your condition. Researchers are also working on new medications that will help change

About ten to twenty percent of the world population have eczema. About 27 percent of infants whose mothers have allergies also suffer from this disorder.

Your doctor and parents can help you cope with eczema.

the way the skin's immune system reacts to environmental triggers.

If you don't respond to any of these treatments, your doctor may have you undergo allergy testing, to determine if your eczema is being caused by a particular food or substance in your

If you're feeling overwhelmed with school work, worried about your social life, or upset about things that are going on in your home, you may be more susceptible to eczema.

A new class of steroid-free drugs has been developed to treat moderately severe eczema. These new medicines, called topical immunomodulators (TIMs), can improve or completely clear eczema in more than 80 percent of patients. Two of these new drugs, called Elidel and Protopic, are available now.

environment. If this proves to be the case, then you will have to take steps to avoid whatever is causing the allergic reaction.

A doctor or dermatologist will be able to help you live with your condition, but there are also steps that you can take to make your life easier. Here are a few tips for living with eczema:

- Don't expose your skin to water any more than you can help. Since water washes away the sebum from your skin (see chapter 1), too much water can dry out your skin and make it more susceptible to eczema. Take short, warm (not hot) showers or baths, don't stay in the swimming pool for more than a few minutes at a time, and wear gloves if you are washing the dishes or doing any other activity that means your hands will be in the water for any length of time.
- Avoid strong soaps, detergents, and household cleaners, as well as anything else you know triggers your eczema.
- Try not to get either chilled or overheated. Becoming sweaty and overheated can trigger eczema—and so can extreme cold.
- Use a moisturizer that doesn't contain fragrance (like petroleum jelly) to keep your skin from becoming irritated.

If you are tested for allergies to foods and other substances, your skin will be pricked with an extract of the substance, and then the doctor will see if your skin reacts. This is useful for determining the more common allergies—but there are literally thousands of substances in the environment that may trigger an allergic reaction in some people, so no doctor can test for everything.

- Don't scratch! It's hard to resist the urge to scratch—but try to remind yourself that every time you itch yourself, your fingernails are breaking the surface of your skin, allowing bacteria to enter, which will make your condition that much worse.
- Wear cotton, and avoid wools. Soft natural fabric is less likely to irritate your skin.
- Practice relaxation techniques; find ways to avoid and dispel the stress in your life. Stress can make you itch!
- Exercise. You may be tempted to avoid exercise, because sweating can trigger a rash—but exercise is a good way to vent the stress and frustrated energy that can lead to bouts of itching. Try to engage in activities on cool days or in an air-conditioned facility where your skin can cool and dry off while you're working out.
- Follow your doctor's or dermatologist's directions. Always take your medications exactly as you've been told.
- If you use makeup, find brands that don't contain fragrance or dyes. These will be less likely to irritate your skin. A dermatologist will also be able to recommend the brands that are best for your condition.

Always take medications on time. Follow your doctor's instructions.

Unfortunately, there's no cure for eczema. But there is good news: most teens who have eczema find that it goes away (or at least gets a whole lot better) by the time they're twenty-five. In the meantime, don't let your itch control your entire life. There

Itchy Rashes

are lots of teens out there who are going through the very same thing. And the more involved you are in interesting activities, the less time you'll have to scratch!

Psoriasis

If you are a teenager with an itchy condition, chances are you don't have psoriasis, since this disease is more likely to occur in adults. However, a few teens do get psoriasis.

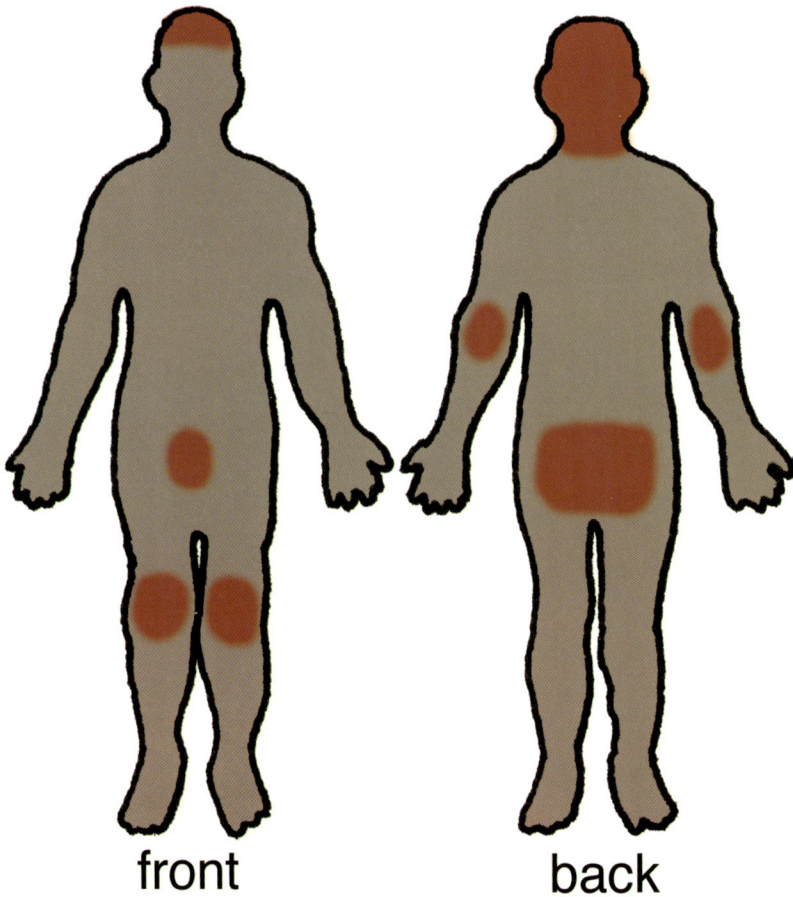

front   back

Psoriasis is most apt to occur on these spots.

Psoriasis is a **CHRONIC** skin condition that causes the skin to be scaly and inflamed. The outer layer of skin cells reproduce faster than normal and pile up on the skin's surface, causing patches of thick red skin covered with silvery scales. These itchy patches are most apt to occur on the elbows, knees, scalp, lower back, palms, soles, and face, but they can show up anywhere on the skin, including fingernails and toenails. When the skin on joints is affected, the skin may crack, and bending and moving may become painful and difficult. Some people with psoriasis also have inflamed joints that cause arthritis-like symptoms; this condition is called psoriatic arthritis.

Researchers believe that psoriasis, like eczema, is caused by a disorder in the immune system. A type of white blood cell, called a T cell, normally protects the skin against infection and disease—but when a person has psoriasis, the T cells release too much of a substance called cytokines, triggering inflammation and skin buildup.

Although psoriasis is caused by something amiss in the immune system, like eczema, certain substances and environmental conditions may cause flare-ups. Changes in temperature, stress, dry skin, infections, and certain medicines may all trigger outbreaks of psoriasis.

Because psoriasis often looks similar to other skin disorders, it can be difficult to diagnose. A **PATHOLOGIST** may perform a **BIOPSY** in order to be certain about exactly what is going on in the skin. Once psoriasis has been definitely diagnosed, a doctor's

Itchy Rashes

treatment plan will be based on the severity of the disease, how much skin is involved, the type of psoriasis (there are five sub-types), and how the individual responds to initial treatments. Most doctors will follow three steps:

1. Prescribe a topical treatment (medicine that is applied externally to the skin). These include corticosteroids, calcipotriene (a SYNTHETIC form of vitamin D), coal tar, salicylic acid (which helps remove scales), and tazarotene (women should use birth control while using this medication, as it can cause birth defects).
2. Have the patient undergo light treatments (phototherapy). Ultraviolet light causes T cells to die, which reduces inflammation and slows the overgrowth of skin cells that causes scales. Nonburning exposure to sunlight or a light box can help many people with psoriasis.
3. Prescribe oral medicines or injections.

If step 1 alone will work, the doctor won't proceed to step 2; and if step 2 works, the doctor will stop there. The goal is to use as little medication as possible to bring relief.

However, over time, a person may become RESISTANT to certain treatments; in other words, medicine that once worked no longer does. Doctors may try to switch treatments every year or every two years, or they may combine therapies.

As researchers gain a better understanding of the immune system, they are also developing new drug treatments for this disease. In January 2002, the FOOD AND DRUG ADMINISTRATION (FDA) approved a new drug called Enbrel® (etanercept) which may be helpful for treating psoriasis. This and other similar drugs block the cytokines' action that causes psoriasis's inflammation. Other drugs are being developed to block inflammation. These

drugs can help for people with psoriasis, but like any drug, they may also have serious SIDE EFFECTS.

If you think you may have psoriasis, be sure to talk to your doctor. Chances are you have another, less serious skin condition. But if you do have psoriasis, don't give up hope. Your dermatologist can help you find ways to live with it—and ongoing research is focusing on developing new treatments for this chronic condition.

The fungus that causes athlete's foot is picked up by bare feet from pools and public showers.

Athlete's Foot

During the summer, Charlene practically lived at her town's pool. She loved to swim, she loved to lie in the sun, and she loved to hang out with her friends by the pool. All winter long, she looked forward to warm weather, and when spring came, she counted the days until the pool opened. But this year when Charlene went to the pool, she picked up something she didn't love—an itchy, burning feeling between her toes and on the soles of her feet.

Tinea infection is the medical term for skin disorders caused by a fungus, and tinea pedis—athlete's foot—is the most common. As Charlene discovered, this condition doesn't affect only athletes. Anyone who has damp or sweaty feet can pick up the contagious disorder; you're most likely to get it from public showers, gym areas, or pools. The fungi that cause athlete's foot love warm, moist places—and they also like to live in the dead cells of your skin. When they do, the skin on your feet will sting and feel itchy, and your skin may flake or crack. If untreated, bacteria can enter these cracks, causing infection. In some cases, the condition can spread to other parts of the body through scratching or from clothing or bedding.

You can avoid catching athlete's foot by never going barefoot in public areas; wear waterproof shoes or thong sandals whenever you take a shower after gym or when walking around a public pool. Keeping your feet as dry as possible at all times will also help you avoid athlete's foot. Try not to wear

Healthy Skin

Imidazole drugs combat fungal infections by attacking the fungi's cell walls, inhibiting their growth and reproduction. Medicines containing clotrimazole and miconazole (for example, Lotrimin®) are sold over the counter. Another imidazole drug, itraconazole (Sporanox®) is available in capsule form. Stronger, prescription medications include allylamines, griseofulvin, terbinafine, and itraconazole.

the same shoes all the time (that way the sweat in your shoes can dry out between wearings), and wear sneakers that have small ventilation holes to help keep your feet dry. Choose socks made of natural fibers (like cotton or wool) instead of polyester, nylon, or other synthetic materials. Don't share towels or washcloths with your friends, as the fungus can be transmitted on the fabric.

But if you do pick up athlete's foot, it's not the end of the world. Over-the-counter creams, powders, or sprays may take care of your problem. If not, consult your doctor. She will be able to quickly diagnose athlete's foot just by looking at the affected skin, and then she can prescribe a stronger antifungal cream or spray, or even a pill that's taken orally. But if you think you have athlete's foot, don't try to ignore it. Serious infections can be difficult to treat, and they may recur for years.

No matter what causes it, having a red, itchy rash on your skin is no fun. It can be embarrassing, and the itch can drive you crazy. But as a young adult, you can take steps to care for yourself, so that you're no longer a total victim to your body's discomfort. Do whatever you can to help yourself—including asking your parents and your doctor for help.

4

Bumps and Patches: Other Skin Conditions

When Lisa was sixteen, she noticed a strange white patch on her arm. "Maybe you have leprosy," her older brother teased. "Maybe it's the creeping crud," her younger brother added.

"Soon you'll turn completely white, like something that crawled out from under a rock."

Lisa's eyes burned with tears of anger and embarrassment. She wanted to throw something at her brothers; instead, she stormed out of the house and shot baskets in the driveway. The exercise helped her feel better—and she forgot about the white patch on her arm. It would go away eventually, she told herself.

But about a month later, Lisa noticed another white patch on her neck, and then another one on the back of her hand. "What's wrong with me?" she asked her mother.

Her mother made an appointment with their family doctor, who was able to quickly make a diagnosis. Lisa had vitiligo. The good news was it wasn't a dangerous condition; it wouldn't make Lisa sick or cause more serious symptoms. The bad news was it wasn't going to go away.

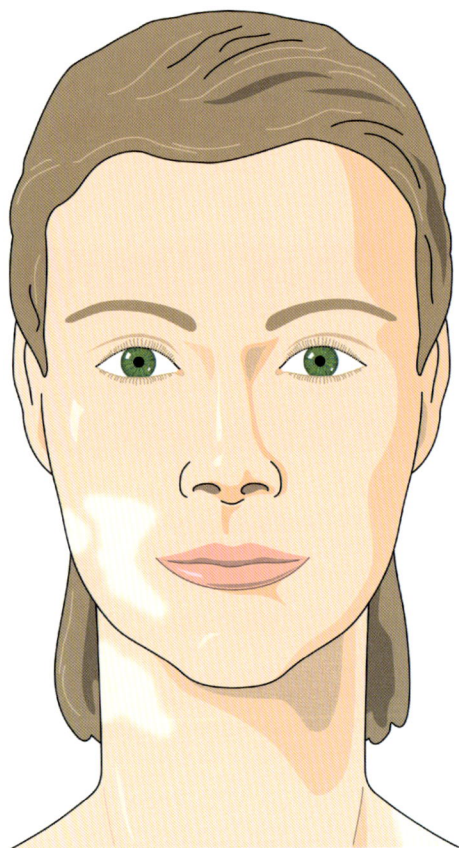

Healthy Skin

Vitiligo can also affect the mucous membranes (the tissues inside the mouth, nose, genital, and rectal areas) and the hair. Hair that grows from areas affected by vitiligo is usually white.

Vitiligo

Vitiligo (pronounced vit-ill-EYE-go) is a pigmentation disorder. The cells in the skin that make pigment, the melanocytes (see chapter 1), die, and white patches appear on different parts of the body.

What Causes Vitiligo?

Doctors aren't sure what causes this condition, but researchers have a few theories. ANTIBODIES may destroy a person's own melanocytes, somehow "mistaking" them for a germ or foreign substance. Or the melanocytes, for some reason, may destroy themselves. Physical or emotional stress (like a bad sunburn or the depression and anxiety caused by family problems) may also trigger vitiligo. Some scientists have found evidence to suggest that vitiligo is caused by a nerve disorder.

Although scientists do not know exactly what causes vitiligo, they do know that it can sometimes be hereditary; children whose parents have this disorder are more apt to develop vitiligo as well. Heredity cannot totally explain vitiligo, however, because even though children whose parents have vitiligo are more susceptible to the disorder, most of these children will never develop vitiligo—and most people with vitiligo have no family history of the condition.

Researchers also know that vitiligo sometimes coincides with certain AUTOIMMUNE DISEASES. People who have a form of

autoimmune disease—for instance, HYPERTHYROIDISM, ADRENAL INSUFFICIENCY, ALOPECIA AREATA, or PERNICIOUS ANEMIA—are more apt to have vitiligo. However, most people who have vitiligo have no other autoimmune disease.

Vitiligo's Symptoms

Although the causes of vitiligo are mysterious, the symptoms are obvious—white patches on the skin. These areas of DEPIGMENTATION are more apt to appear on areas exposed to the sun, like the hands, arms, face, and lips, but white patches are also likely form in the armpits and the groin, as well as around the mouth, eyes, nostrils, and navel.

Vitiligo usually appears in one of three patterns:

- *Focal pattern.* The depigmentation is limited to one area or possibly only a few areas.
- *Segmental pattern.* The white patches develop on only one side of the body.
- *Generalized pattern.* Areas of depigmentation show up on various parts of the body.

People with vitiligo often have white patches of hair on their heads or in their beards, or they may have white eyelashes or

Healthy Skin

eyebrows. People with dark skin may notice that the skin inside their mouths also lacks color.

Vitiligo is usually progressive; eventually, over time, the white patches will spread to other parts of the body. However, this is not true for everyone. Each person is affected by vitiligo differently. One person may have only a few white patches her entire life, while someone else may find his white patches quickly spread to new areas, and yet another individual may notice that her areas of depigmentation spread very slowly, over the space of many years. Some people with this skin condition have noticed that new white patches sometimes appear after a period of emotional or physical stress.

Diagnosing Vitiligo

If you suspect you have vitiligo, you should consult with your doctor. He will usually begin with questions about your family and personal medical history. He may ask you questions like these:

- Does anyone else in your family have vitiligo?
- Do you or anyone else in your family have an autoimmune disease?
- Has anyone in your family developed gray hair before the age of thirty-five?
- Did you have a rash, sunburn, or other skin trauma at the site of the white patches two to three months before you noticed the depigmentation?
- Are you very sensitive to the sun?
- Are you experiencing any unusual emotional stress?
- Do you have any other medical conditions?

Your doctor may also take a small sample of the affected skin and run various tests on it. She may take a blood sample as well to check your blood-cell count and your THYROID function. Another blood test can help determine if you have another autoimmune disease by looking for autoantibodies (antibodies that attack a part of your own body). Sometimes, your doctor may also recommend an eye examination to rule out uveitis, an inflammation of part of the eye.

Treatment Options for Vitiligo

There is no permanent cure for vitiligo, but various therapies can help restore skin function and make white patches less noticeable. These therapies usually take a long time—as long as six to eighteen months—and each person will respond differently. Here are some of the most common treatments:

- TOPICAL STEROID THERAPY. Corticosteroids are a group of drugs that contain chemicals similar to the hormones produced by the adrenal glands, and these medications may help return color to white patches, particularly if they're used early in the disease. You will need to apply the corticosteroid cream to the white patches for at least three months before you will see any results. This is the safest and simplest treatment, but it can cause side effects such as skin shrinkage and streaks or lines on the skin. If your doctor prescribes a topical steroid cream to treat your vitiligo, he will closely monitor you for any of these side effects.
- NARROW BAND ULTRAVIOLET "B" THERAPY. Recently, special lamps that give off small amounts of ultraviolet B light have become popular for treating Vitiligo. This type of therapy is called Narrow Band Ultraviolet "B"

Healthy Skin

Therapy, or nbUVB. This treatment has been found to be effective for a majority of patients, and since there are no other medications involved in the therapy, there are very few side effects. These lamps can also be placed in patients' homes so that they do not have to go to the doctor's office to receive the treatment.

- DEPIGMENTATION. For people who have vitiligo on more than half of their bodies, the best option may be to fade the rest of the skin to match the already white areas. This is accomplished by applying a drug called monobenzyl ether of hydroquinone twice a day to the normally pigmented areas until they match the depigmented patches. This is a permanent treatment that can never be reversed; if you choose this treatment, you will be abnormally sensitive to sunlight for the rest of your life. Other possible side effects include itching, dry skin, or darkening of the membrane that covers the whites of your eyes.

- SURGICAL THERAPIES, INCLUDING SKIN GRAFTS AND ME-LANOCYTE TRANSPLANTS. If you only have a small patch of vitiligo, it may be possible to graft normal, pigmented skin from somewhere else on your body to the white patch. However, there is a risk of infection and scarring, and the procedure is expensive and time-consuming. Another surgical therapy, melanocyte transplants, involves growing cell cultures taken from the person's normal skin; then when the melanocytes in the skin culture have multiplied, the doctor transplants them into the depigmented patches. Many doctors consider all these surgical treatments to be experimental, since their effectiveness and side effects have not been thoroughly researched.

Coping with the Emotional Impact of Vitiligo

Having white patches on your skin can be embarrassing. Teens are especially apt to be hypersensitive to any changes in their appearance, and as a result, this skin disorder can be emotionally devastating for adolescents. Their embarrassment and shame may lead to depression and anxiety.

If you or another teenager you know has vitiligo, you should be aware that there are positive steps you can take to help cope with this skin disorder:

- Find a doctor who is knowledgeable about vitiligo. She should be able to help you understand your condition—and she should be a good listener who provides emotional support.
- Learn as much as you can about vitiligo from your doctor, from the library, from the Internet. The more you know, the more you can participate in determining what treatment choices are best for you—and the more control you will have over your own life.
- Let your doctor, your parents, a school counselor, or some other adult know if you are experiencing depression or anxiety over your condition. They can refer you to a mental health expert who will be able to help you better cope with your emotions.
- Talk with other people who are going through the same thing. The National Vitiligo Foundation (see "For More Information" at the back of this book) can refer you to local support groups where you can talk with other individuals who are experiencing the same thing you are.
- Share your feelings with your family and friends. Emotional support is an important part of mental health; you don't need to go through this alone.

Healthy Skin

Researchers are seeking new cures for vitiligo and other skin disorders.

The University of Colorado is researching families with vitiligo in the United States and the United Kingdom, hoping to determine the specific gene or genes that causes individuals to be susceptible to this condition. Over 2,400 people with vitiligo have been involved in this study.

- Wear sunscreen that provides protection against UVA and UVB forms of ultraviolet light. (Read the labels carefully.) This will help protect white patches from sunburn and long-term damage, and it also minimizes tanning, which will make the contrast between the white patches and your normal skin less noticeable.
- You may want to experiment with using cosmetics to conceal the most obvious white patches. Your doctor or someone else who is experiencing vitiligo may be able to recommend which brands will work best. Stains and self-tanning products often work well for covering up depigmented areas.

As a young adult, you are no longer totally dependent on others for your care and well-being; you are old enough now to take responsibility for your emotions, and you don't have to allow vitiligo to overwhelm your entire life. Take action!

Staph Infections

Like everyone else his age, Jason got pimples on his face and shoulders. But one morning he noticed a bump on his neck that was different than any pimple he had ever seen. And the bump just kept growing, until it was huge and red and sore. When the school nurse took a look at it, she said it was a boil, an infection caused by a bacteria called staphylococcus (pronounced sta-fuh-low-KAH-kus).

These germs—usually called "staph" for short—are often on the skin without causing any harm. But if the skin is broken, staph germs can enter the skin and cause a number of different infections, including:

Healthy Skin

- boils, also referred to as abscesses or furuncles (pronounced FYOOR-unk-ills), where infection affects the sebaceous glands and subcutaneous tissue (see chapter 1)
- folliculitis, an infection of the hair follicle that sometimes leads to a boil
- impetigo, a bacterial infection that kids and teens sometimes get where sores with a honey-colored crust form on the skin, usually around the nose and mouth
- scalded skin syndrome, which mostly affects babies and younger children
- toxic shock syndrome
- cellulitis

Treating Staph Infections

If you have an area of red, swollen, or painful skin, you should call your doctor, especially if you have a fever or if you see white, pus-filled spots on your skin. If you have a small staph infection that only affects a small part of your skin, your doctor may suggest you wash the infected skin with an antibacterial cleanser, apply a topical antibacterial ointment, and cover the skin with a clean bandage. If your infection is more severe and you are running a fever, your doctor will probably prescribe an antibiotic to kill the germs causing the infection.

In the meantime, in order to avoid spreading the infection to other areas of skin on your body or to friends and family, be careful not to touch the infected skin. A heating pad or a hot water bottle may help relieve the pain, and you may want to take pain relievers like acetaminophen (Tylenol®) or ibuprofen (Motrin® or Advil®).

Most boils will heal by themselves in ten to twenty days, but antibiotic treatment will help them heal faster and prevent the spread of infection to other skin areas.

Preventing Staph Infections

There's no way to avoid coming in contact with staph bacteria: it's everywhere. The best way to prevent this common germ from infecting your skin is to bathe or shower daily and wash your hands often. If you have a cut or scrape or a rash caused by some other skin condition, be sure to keep it clean and covered, and use an antibiotic ointment to help it heal without the complications staph bacteria can cause.

Other Annoying Bumps and Marks

Warts

Did you ever hear the old wives' tale that you can catch warts from handling a toad? Actually, warts are tiny skin infections caused by human papilloma viruses (HPV). You can't catch it from toads—but warts can spread. If you have a wart, don't pick it or scratch, as that releases the virus, causing the warts to spread. Over-the-counter medications containing a special kind of acid (one example is Compound W®) can help you get rid of warts. If you have a particularly large, deep-rooted wart, you may want to consult a doctor. She may decide to use a local anesthesia and then burn or freeze away the wart tissues.

stye

boils, carbuncles

sinusitis

furuncles

hematogenous spread

endocarditis

pneumonia

impetigo

emesis

diarrhea

toxic shock syndrome

uti
cystitis

scalded skin syndrome

osteomyelitis

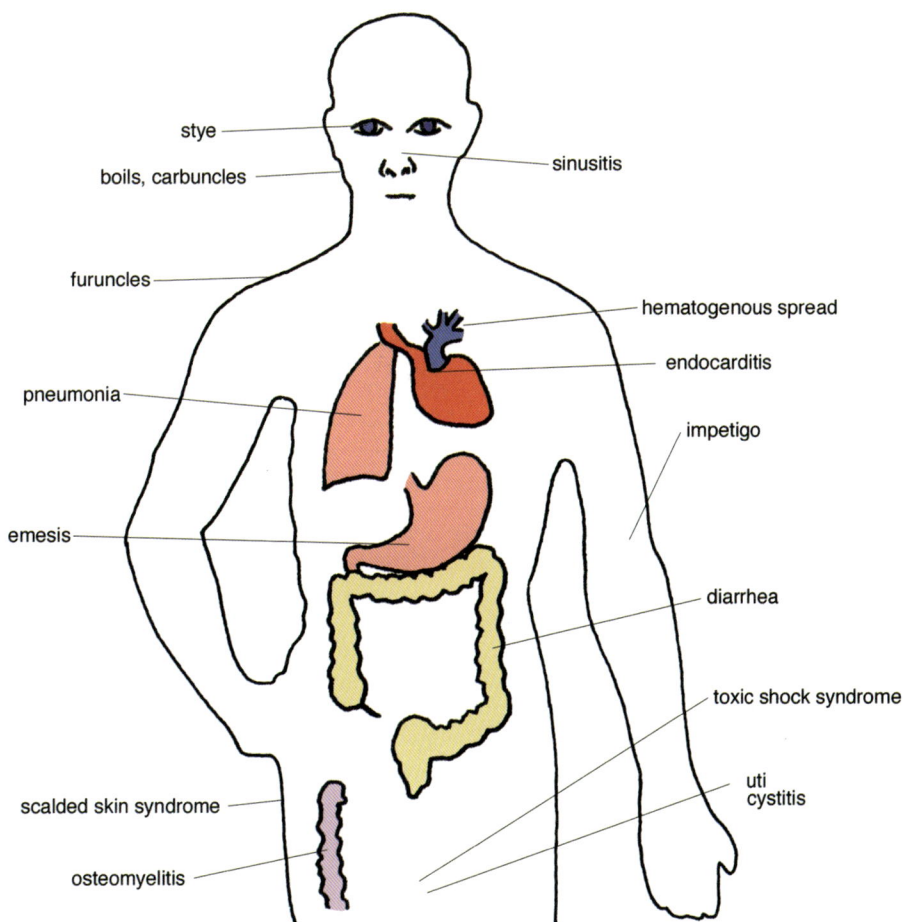

Staph infections can affect many parts of the body.

About 30 percent of all healthy people have staph bacteria in their noses. Staph begins growing on most people before they're even a week old! And in most cases, our skin will act as an effective barrier against this germ, protecting us from infection.

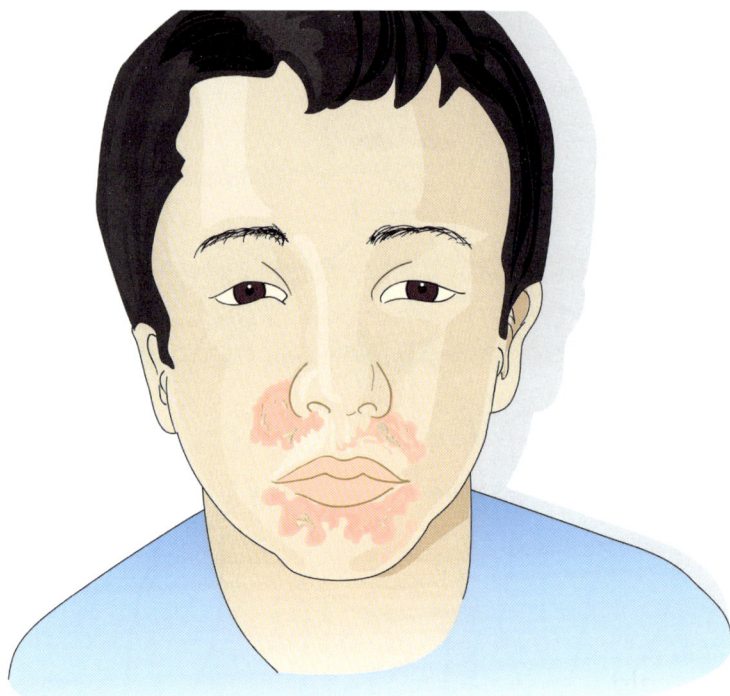

Impetigo is a staph infection that causes crusty sores around the mouth and nose.

Cold Sores

These sore blisters form on the lips and the sensitive tissues inside your nose. They're caused by a type of herpes virus (herpes simplex, which is the same as the herpes virus that is sexually transmitted), and they're contagious from person to person. This means if you have a cold sore, you'd better take a break from kissing your boyfriend or girlfriend—and you should also avoid sharing stuff like lip balm, drinks, or toothbrushes.

Once you get herpes simplex, the virus stays in your body forever. You won't have cold sores all the time, but you'll be susceptible to them whenever you're physically or emotionally stressed (like if you're sick with the flu or a cold or if it's finals week and

Healthy Skin

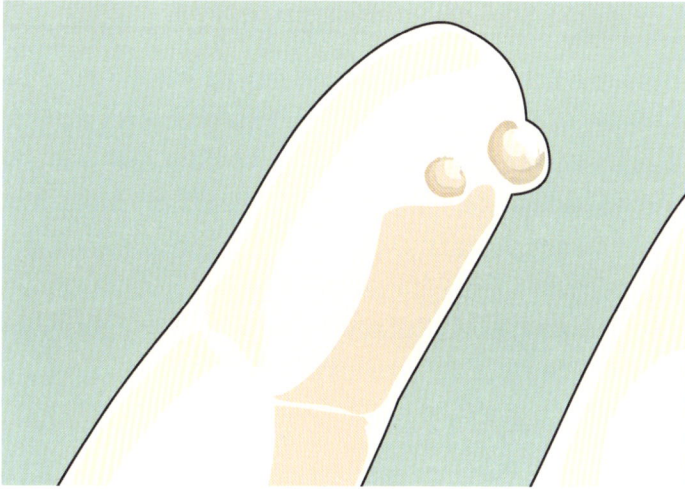

Warts are caused by a virus.

you've stayed up five nights in a row to study). Too much sun can also cause cold sores to flare up, so if you've had a cold sore, be sure to use lip balm that contains a sunscreen.

Cold sores will usually go away by themselves in a week or two, but over-the-counter medication is available that will speed up their healing. While you're waiting for them to go away, here are some tips for living with them:

This is what a herpes virus looks like (magnified many thousands of times).

Canker sores are different from cold sores. Unlike cold sores, canker sores occur on the skin inside your mouth (on your tongue and the insides of your cheeks and lips), and they are not contagious. Women are more apt to get canker sores than men, and women are apt to get them at certain times during their menstrual cycle, indicating that there may be a connection between female hormones and canker sores. Dietary deficiencies, such as not getting enough iron or vitamin B12, may also contribute to some instances of canker sores.

- Stay away from sour, acidic foods (like orange juice, lemonade, and tomato sauce) and salty foods, which can irritate cold sores.
- Don't pick at cold sores. This will only make them take longer to heal, and you may introduce staph bacteria or other germs, which can lead to a new and worse infection.
- Suck on popsicles or ice cubes to help ease the discomfort of cold sores.
- If your cold sores are very painful, take a painkiller like acetaminophen or ibuprofen.

Stretch Marks

Some teens, especially girls, may notice fine white or purplish lines on their skin. These lines form when the tissue under your skin tears from stretching; that's why pregnant women get them on their stomachs, but teenagers can get them too during times of rapid growth. According to their advertisements, some creams and ointments will remove stretch marks—but

Healthy Skin

the truth is the only way to permanently remove these marks is with microdermabrasion (see chapter 2). Most stretch marks aren't very noticeable, though, and they usually fade and become less noticeable with time.

Your skin is right out there where everybody sees it, so when you get patches and bumps on your skin, you may feel embarrassed and ashamed. The truth is, though, nobody's skin is perfect. Everyone in the world has experienced one kind of skin condition or another. So if you're dealing with one right now, you're not alone.

Do what you can to take control of your skin condition, whatever it is. Don't be afraid to ask for help from your parents or a medical professional. And remember—although you may feel as though that bump on your chin or patch on your cheek is the end of the world, it's really not!

5

When the Sun Becomes an Enemy: Protecting Yourself Against Skin Cancer

Almost everyone in North America likes to have suntanned skin. It's the style. What's more, we connect paleness with being unhealthy, while we think of people who are tanned as being healthy and outdoorsy. If you leaf through the pages of any magazine like *Seventeen*, *People*, or *Sports Illustrated*, you'll

Up until the twentieth century, pale white skin was considered desirable throughout the United States, Canada, and most of Europe. If you were tan, you had obviously been performing labor in the sun—which meant you were not a member of the wealthy upper class. The whiter your skin, the more elegant, sophisticated, and rich you appeared. In the eighteenth century, some members of the nobility even powdered their faces in order to make their skin appear as light as possible.

notice that most models, actors, and athletes have tanned skin. And summer just wouldn't be summer if you didn't hang out at the pool or beach and soak up some rays.

In the minds of most North Americans, rainy days are sad but sunny days are happy. We connect sunshine with feeling cheerful, and we think of the sun as wearing a smiling kindly face, the way it does sometimes in children's picture books. And it's true, life on Earth depends on the sun's light—but we'd do well to remember that the sun is a burning ball of flame, and its immense power is not always kind to us earthlings. Sometimes, the sun's light can be destructive. Our skin is the part of our bodies most vulnerable to the sun's harmful touch.

The sun's rays contain two types of ultraviolet radiation that reach the Earth's surface: UVA and UVB. UVB radiation can burn the skin's upper layers (the epidermis), but UVA penetrates deeper, down to the melanocytes in the dermis. The melanocytes react by making even more brown pigment than usual to protect your skin from the sun. The melanin (the pigment) acts like a sunshade or an umbrella, protecting each cell from the sun's damage.

Healthy Skin

This eighteenth-century woman's white skin indicates she was a member of the upper class.

But the melanin can only protect your skin cells so far. If you continue to expose your skin to UVA and UVB radiation, eventually your skin will begin to age faster than normal. Damaged cells will make your skin look wrinkly or blotchy. You may have brown age spots and leathery sagging skin. You will probably look far older than you really are. Exposure to the sun is one of the big reasons why older people look different from younger people.

The sun's rays don't only contribute to the aging process, however; they can also cause skin cancer. In many areas of the world, including the United States, skin cancer has now become an EPIDEMIC. While the numbers of new cases of other kinds of cancer are either leveling off or actually decreasing, the number of cases of skin cancer is growing. In the past, this potentially deadly disease affected mostly adults who were fifty or older—but now, dermatologists report that they are seeing more and more people in their twenties who have skin cancer.

There are three main kinds of skin cancer:

· malignant melanoma
· basal cell carcinoma
· squamous cell carcinoma

Healthy Skin

An abnormal skin growth called actinic keratosis is a pre-cancer that may eventually turn into skin cancer.

Melanoma

This form of skin cancer is the most deadly, but it is also the least common. It looks like a patch of brown and black skin, or like

DERMATOLOGISTS SPEAK OF SIX DIFFERENT SKIN TYPES:

Type I	blond hair/ very white skin	always burns/ never tans
Type II	white skin	always burns/tans a little
Type III	light skin	sometimes burns/sometimes tans
Type IV	light brown skin	burns a little/always tans
Type V	brown skin	rarely burns/tans darkly
Type VI	dark hair/ dark brown skin	never burns/tans darkly

Which type of skin do you have?

a multicolored patch of red, blue, and white. The patch's edges are usually notched or scalloped, and it is generally larger than a quarter of an inch across (6 mm). Although melanoma is a very serious disease, it can often be cured if you receive treatment in the early stages. Without early diagnosis and treatment, however, the cancer may METASTASIZE (spread) to other areas of the body, such as the lungs, liver, bones, brain, or lymph nodes. When this happens, the chance of complete recovery is less likely.

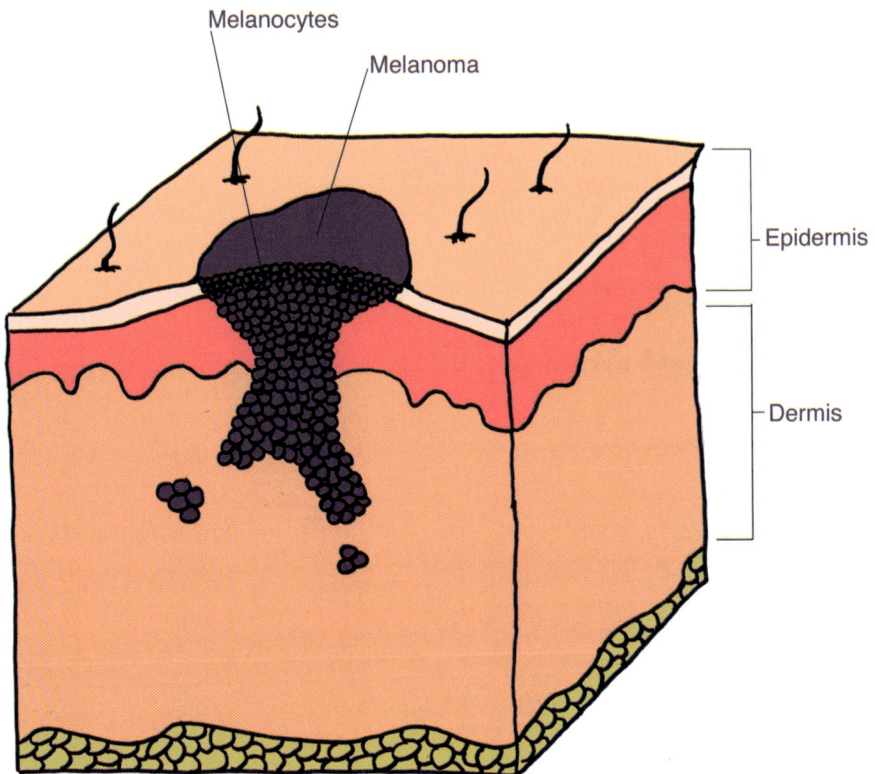

Healthy Skin

Men are more apt to develop melanomas on the shoulders, hips, head, or neck. In women, melanomas are more likely to develop on the lower legs and lower back.

People who have fair skin that burns or freckles easily have a greater risk of developing melanoma. This serious form of skin cancer is also more common in areas where the Earth receives large amounts of ultraviolet radiation from the sun; places like

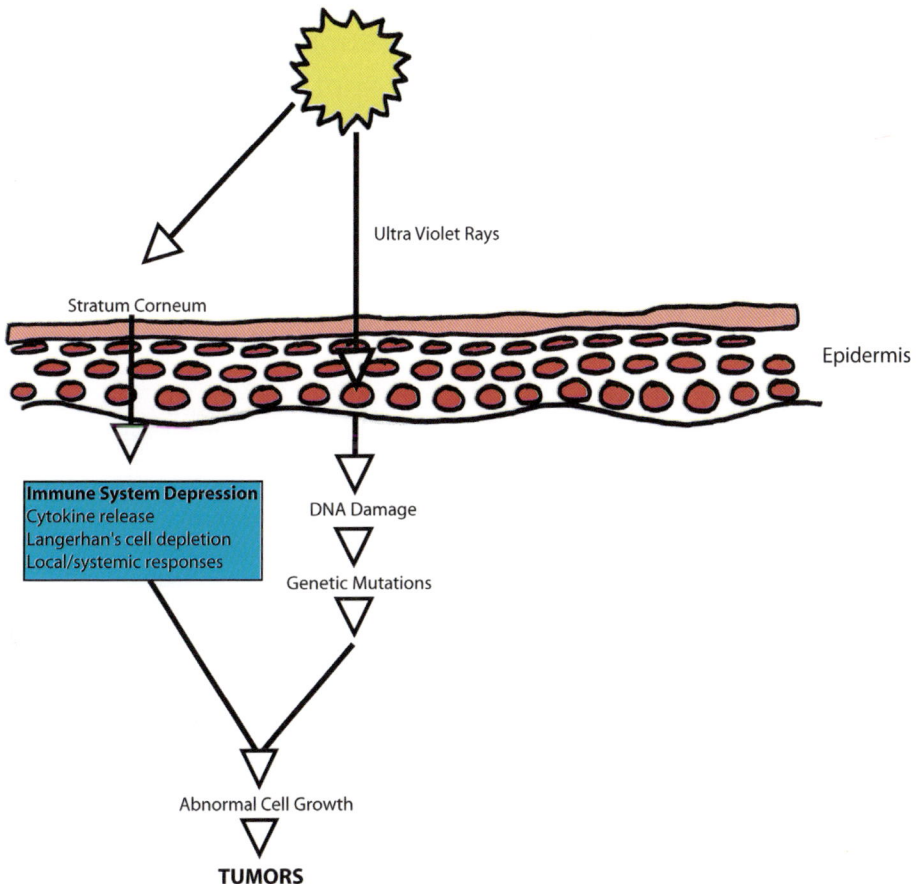

Ultra Violet Rays

Stratum Corneum

Epidermis

Immune System Depression
Cytokine release
Langerhan's cell depletion
Local/systemic responses

DNA Damage

Genetic Mutations

Abnormal Cell Growth

TUMORS

WHEN THE SUN BECOMES AN ENEMY

the American Southwest and areas of Africa near the equator have higher incidences of melanoma.

There are several other risk factors for melanoma:

- A family history of melanoma. The susceptibility to this form of skin cancer may be hereditary. People who have two or more close relatives who have had melanoma have a greater chance of developing it themselves.
- Unusual looking moles.
- More than fifty ordinary moles.
- Previous melanoma. If you've had melanoma once, you're more apt to get it again.
- A history of severe, blistering sunburns. Anyone who as a child had one or more bad sunburns (where the skin

Signs of melanoma:

- a skin growth that increases in size and looks pearly, tan, brown, black, pink, red, or multicolored
- any mole that is larger than a pencil eraser, or a mole that changes color or texture, grows larger, or becomes irregular in shape
- a spot or growth that does heal but continues to itch, hurt, crust over, or bleed
- an open sore that lasts for more than four weeks, or a sore that heals and then reopens
- a scaly or crusty bump that feels tender and prickly

If you see any of these spots or bumps on your skin, consult your doctor right away. Early diagnosis and treatment can make the difference between life and death!

The sun is not always a friend!

WHEN THE SUN BECOMES AN ENEMY

blistered) also has greater odds of getting melanoma as an adult. That's why it's so important that children wear sunscreen whenever they're in the sun. But adults should also be careful not to get severe sunburns, as they too can become more susceptible to this cancer.

- A weakened immune system. The drugs given after an organ transplant, certain cancers, and **HIV/AIDS** virus can affect the body's ability to protect itself, increasing the risk of melanoma (as well as other diseases).

But just because you have a greater susceptibility to melanoma and other skin cancers, doesn't mean you're doomed to develop this disease. If you have one or more of the risk factors listed on pages 86–88, that just means you should be all the more careful to do what you can to take care of yourself.

Basal Cell Carcinoma

This form of skin cancer is more common than melanoma, but it has a higher cure rate. It can take various forms: a red patch; a shiny pink, red, or white bump; a crusty open sore that won't heal; or a scar-like dent.

Squamous Cell Carcinoma

Like basal cell carcinoma, this form of skin cancer is more common and less deadly than melanoma, but it too can be potentially fatal. It usually takes the form of a scaly red patch, an open

9000 FT
Above Sea Level

45% More UV

8000 FT
Above Sea Level

40% More UV

7000 FT
Above Sea level

35% More UV

6000 FT
Above Sea Level

30% More UV

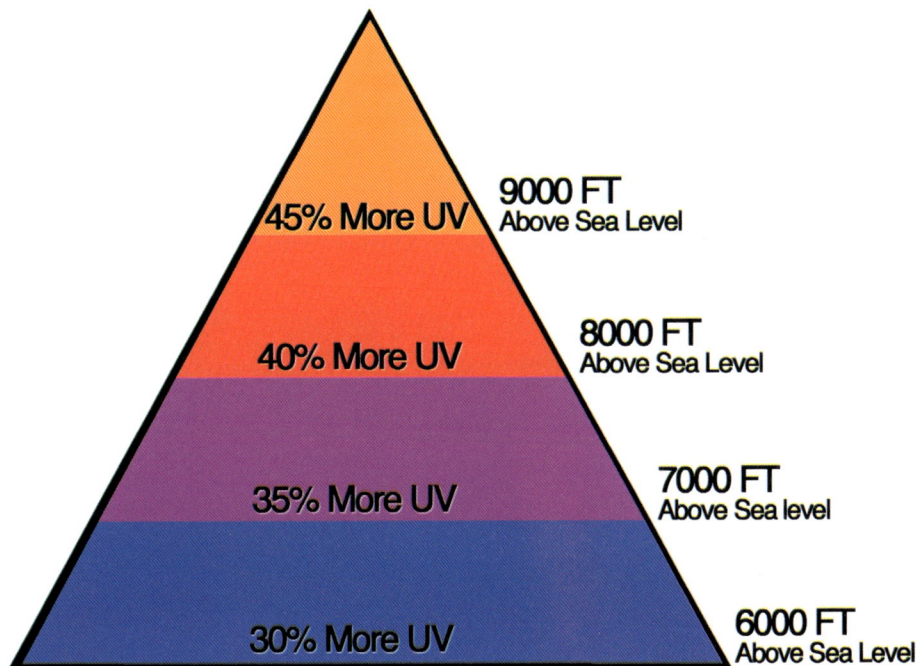

The higher your elevation, the more you are exposed to ultraviolet rays, and the more care you need to take to protect your skin from the sun.

sore, or raised and sometimes bleeding wart-like growth; whatever its form, it doesn't heal and go away.

Skin Cancer Treatments

The word "cancer" is really scary to most people. Because it's so frightening, sometimes people try not to even think about it, and they ignore any warning signs they might have. But cancer doesn't have to be deadly if you take action early.

If you develop a suspicious spot on your skin, see your doctor right away. If she thinks it might be skin cancer, you will be given a local anesthetic, and a small sample of the affected skin will be cut off and tested for cancerous cells.

WHEN THE SUN BECOMES AN ENEMY

If it turns out you do have skin cancer, chances are your treatment will involve some kind of surgery. Many skin cancers can simply be cut away from the skin. In some cases, the cancer is completely removed at the same time as the biopsy is taken, and no further treatment is needed. If you do need additional surgery, your doctor will choose from the following list the treatment that is best for you:

- CURETTAGE AND ELECTRODESICCATION. This is one of the most common forms of surgery used to treat skin cancers. After a local anesthetic numbs the affected area, the cancer is removed with a sharp, spoon-shaped instrument called a curette. An electric current is then applied to the wound in a process called electrodesiccation. This helps control bleeding and kills any cancer cells remaining around the edge of the treated skin. If you have this form of surgery, you will probably have a flat, white scar after the wound heals.

- MOHS SURGERY. During this treatment, the cancer is shaved off one thin layer at a time, and each layer is checked under a microscope until no cancerous cells remain. This technique is designed to remove all of the cancerous tissues and as little of the healthy tissue as possible. A surgeon may choose this method if he is not sure of the shape and depth of the cancer, and it is a good technique to use with large tumors or with skin cancer that is in a hard-to-treat place.

- CRYOSURGERY. Small skin cancers and the precancerous condition called actinic keratosis can be treated by using extreme cold to kill the abnormal skin cells. Liquid nitrogen is applied to the area, freezing the tissue; as the skin thaws, the dead cells fall off. Sometimes more than one treatment is needed to remove the cancer completely.

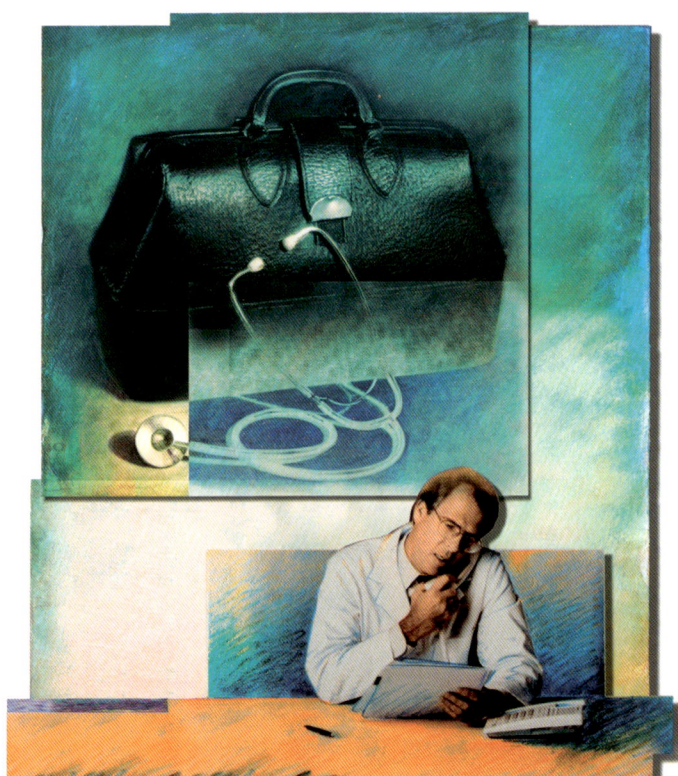

If you think you might have skin cancer, talk to your doctor immediately.

This process doesn't hurt, but afterward you might have some pain and swelling, and you'll usually have a white scar once the area heals.

· LASER THERAPY. A laser is a powerful, narrow beam of light; it can be used to kill and cut away the cancer cells. This technique is usually used for cancers that affect only the outermost layer of skin.

· GRAFTING. This surgical process is used to reduce scarring after another surgery to take out a skin cancer. The

surgeon takes a piece of healthy skin from some other part of your body, and then she uses it to close the wound left when a large skin cancer is removed.

Sometimes, doctors also suggest radiation therapy or chemotherapy to treat skin cancer, or a combination of these treatments may be used. Doctors often use radiation therapy on skin cancer that has developed on areas that are hard to treat surgically (for example, your eyelid, your ear, or the tip of your nose). High-energy rays damage the cancer cells and stop them from growing. Often several treatments are needed, and the radiation may cause a rash or make your skin dry and red. Chemotherapy can be applied as a cream or lotion, usually over

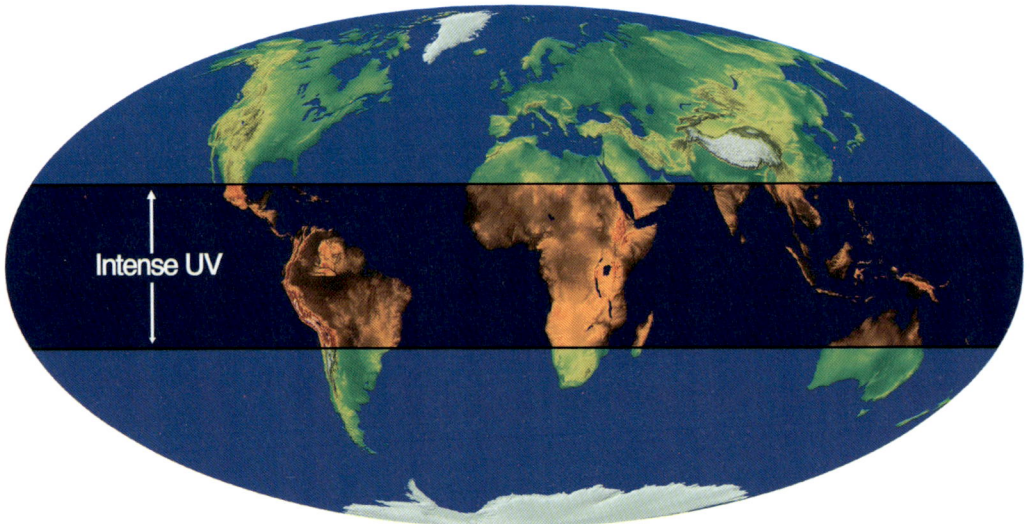

Intense UV

The regions near the equator receive more intense ultraviolet light. People living in these areas (or visiting these areas) need to take extra care to protect their skin from the sun's harmful rays.

Healthy Skin

Researchers are exploring new ways to treat skin cancer:

- Photodynamic therapy uses a combination of laser light and drugs to make the cancer cells sensitive to light.
- Biological therapy or immunotherapy uses the body's natural ability to fight cancer. Interferon and tumor necrosis factor are two types of biological therapy that scientists are studying.

a period of several weeks. This treatment works best with actinic keratosis (precancerous skin growths) and with skin cancer that only affects the top layer of skin.

If you find out you have skin cancer, it's normal to feel scared, but skin cancer doesn't have to be a death sentence. The more you talk to your doctor and educate yourself about your condition, the more you'll be able to handle your fears.

These are some of the questions you might want to talk over with your doctor:

- What types of treatment are available?
- Which treatment will be best for me and why?
- Are there any risks or side effects to treatment?
- How long will the treatment take? How often will I have to come in for treatment?
- How will treatment affect my normal life? Will I have to change what I do every day?
- Will I have a scar?
- What are the chances I will get skin cancer again? How can I protect myself?
- How often will I need a check up after my cancer has been removed?

Although skin cancer is the most common cancer in the United States, it accounts for only one percent of all deaths caused by cancer. That's because skin cancer has a better prognosis (outcome) than most types of cancer. Most cases of skin cancer—85 to 95 percent—can be cured.

Preventing Skin Cancer

Skin cancer can be treated, and usually it can be cured. But it makes sense to do whatever you can to protect yourself from ever getting skin cancer in the first place.

Protecting yourself from skin cancer doesn't mean you have to stay inside all the time, though, and you don't have to wrap yourself in heavy clothes from head to toe either. Being careful to always apply a sunscreen to your skin whenever you go in the sun is one of the best ways to protect yourself, and it won't interfere with your activities or the way you look.

Here are some other tips for avoiding skin cancer:

- Wear sunscreen daily (or use a moisturizer that has sunscreen in it), even on cloudy days. Dermatologists believe that as much as 80 percent of our exposure to the sun's harmful rays happens when we're engaged in everyday life activities—walking down the street, eating lunch outside, or talking with a friend outside the school building. In other words, it's not just when you're lying in the sun by the beach that you have to worry about the radiation that causes skin cancer. Even when you can't see the sun, harmful radiation can penetrate the clouds.
- Use a sunscreen with a sun protection factor (SPF) of at least 15 on an everyday basis. If you'll be spending time in

Healthy Skin

direct sunlight, use a sunscreen with a higher SPF, like SPF 30.

- Check out the ingredients in your sunscreen. Make sure the sunscreen you use blocks both UVA and UVB rays. (You might want to also check that your sunscreen is hypoallergenic and noncomedogenic, so it doesn't cause a

Don't only protect your face when you are out in the sun. Your shoulders and your legs are also susceptible to ultraviolet radiation. That beautiful suntan you're working on is really a sign that your skin is being damaged by the sun's harmful rays.

Healthy Skin

rash or make you get pimples. Water-based sunscreens are better if you have oily skin, and if you have a reaction to one sunscreen, switch to another; not all sunscreens contain the same chemicals.) If you're going to exercise or swim, you might want to use a waterproof sunscreen.

· Use enough sunscreen to make a difference. One ounce (enough to fill the palm of your hand) is usually enough to cover your entire body adequately.

· Apply sunscreen to all parts of your body that are exposed to the sun (don't forget your ears and the backs of your knees), and reapply it every two or three hours (more often if you're swimming or sweating).

· Try not to be in the sun for extended periods between ten in the morning and four in the afternoon. (The sun's rays are strongest and most direct during these hours.)

· Wear a hat with a brim and sunglasses to protect your eyes from the sun's radiation.

· Remember that reflective surfaces can increase the amount of ultraviolet radiation hitting your skin, so you'll need to be extra careful when you're around snow and water.

· If you're taking antibiotics or birth control pills, be aware that you may have increased sensitivity to the sun.

· Don't use sun lamps and tanning beds. Although most sun lamps and tanning beds don't emit UVB radiation (so they shouldn't burn your skin), they do use UVA light— and the UVA radiation is greater than what you'd get

Dermatologists believe that tanning salons are one reason they're treating more patients in their twenties for skin cancer.

North Americans' behaviors, lack of knowledge, and attitudes have contributed to the skin cancer epidemic:

- 31 percent of Americans reported not using sunscreen while 69 percent were occasional users.
- Only one third know that melanoma is a kind of skin cancer that can be caused by overexposure to the sun.
- One out of three teenagers believe that they look better with a tan.

from the sun. This means that if you use a sun lamp or a tanning bed, you're actually absorbing far more harmful radiation than you would in the same amount of time from the sun. You'll make your skin age more quickly, and you put yourself at greater risk for skin cancer.

Healthy Skin

Airbrush tanning is another safe way to get the appearance of a tan. The same chemical found in self-tanners is applied by a salon technician with a spray compressor. The results are more like a natural tan than most self-tanners, but the procedure is usually between $25 and $60.

If you still want to have the bronzed, tanned look that lying in the sun can give you, a sunless self-tanner ("tan-in-a-bottle") is a safe alternative. Self-tanners contain a chemical that OXIDIZES on the skin's outermost layer, giving you the appearance of a suntan. Most self-tanners last anywhere from a few hours to a week, and if you apply them evenly, these creams and sprays can give you a realistic "suntan."

Imagine if somehow we could all see each other's lungs—and it was the fad to show up with the black, damaged lung tissue caused by smoking. The blacker your lungs, the cooler you'd be, while healthy, pink lung tissue would be considered embarrassing. A style like that sounds pretty silly—but our culture's obsession with tanning is just as foolish. The truth is, a suntan is really just visible proof that your skin is being damaged by the sun.

Spending time in the sun is fun, and you may like the way a suntan looks—but is that deep brown glow you get from the sun really worth risking medical treatment, scars, and possibly more serious complications down the road?

6

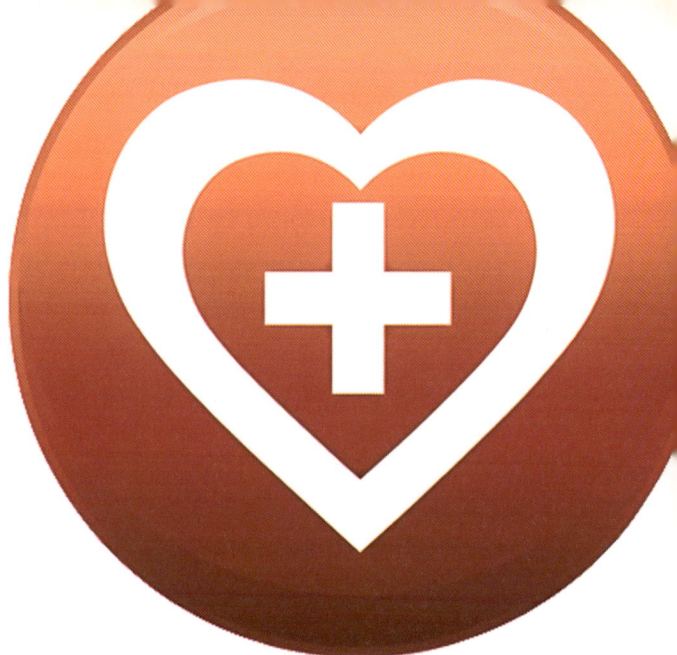

More Ways to Care For Your Skin

Your skin is a strong and durable organ that will serve your body well throughout your life. But it will stay healthy and young-looking longer if you take care of it.

Hygiene

Staying clean is one of the best ways to protect your skin. We've already talked about how dirt and skin oils interact to form

acne (see chapter 2) and how germs can penetrate a break in the skin to cause infection (see chapter 4). Here are a few more tips for keeping your skin clean:

- Bathe or shower every day.
- Use a washcloth or a loofah to remove dead cells from the surface of your skin, but avoid scrubbing so hard that you irritate your skin.
- Avoid using very hot water when washing your skin, as this can dry your skin.
- Use mild soaps that won't dry out your skin. If you have very dry skin on some areas of your body, use soap only on your face, underarms, crotch area, hands, and feet; the rest of you will get sufficiently clean with water alone.

Shaving can damage skin cells, so use shaving cream and a sharp blade.

SKIN CARE MYTHS

MYTH: Cucumbers contain a special ingredient that will help reduce swelling in the skin around your eyes.

FACT: The only special ingredient that cucumbers contain is water. A moist washcloth would do the same trick by cooling and hydrating your skin.

MYTH: You need to get plenty of sleep in order for your skin cells to regenerate themselves.

FACT: Skin repair goes on constantly, day and night, whether you are asleep or awake.

- After washing, use a moisturizing oil or cream. If you have oily skin, use a water-based lotion rather than one that is oil-based.
- Shaving can be hard on your skin. Always use a sharp blade and shaving cream, and shave in the same direction your hairs grow. Electric razors are more apt to irritate skin than straight razors.
- Wear clean clothes every day, especially your socks and underwear.

As a teenager, you may feel as though it's more difficult to stay clean than it used to be. That's because your sweat glands are more active now than when you were younger, and your

A DICTIONARY OF COSMETIC INGREDIENTS

NAME	FUNCTION
sodium laureth sulfate	cleansing and lathering
glycine soja	moisturizer
sodium lauroamphoacetate	cleansing and lathering
PEG-6 caprylic/ capric glycerides	moisturizer/emollient
palm kernel acid	thickener/skin conditioner
magnesium sulfate	thickener
glycerin	moisturizer
cocamide MEA	cleansing and lathering
citric acid	adjusts skin pH
maleated soybean oil	moisturizer/emollient
fragrance	scent
polyquaternium-10	skin conditioner/ emollient
disodium EDTA	chelator
sodium benzoate	preservative

To avoid dry skin, use a moisturizer after shaving your legs.

sweat also has a stronger odor than it used to. Using deodorant daily is a good idea once you notice these changes in your body.

Although deodorant brands like to advertise their differences, the fact is, they all contain similar chemicals. Whether they're sticks, sprays, roll-ons, or creams, they're all about the same—even the ones that say they're made especially for a man or a woman (the only difference is the fragrance). The only real difference is between deodorants and antiperspirants. Deodorants' job is to cover up the odor of sweat, while an antiperspirant works to actually stop or dry up perspiration. Read the labels carefully so you know what you're buying. And don't ever assume that you can skip washing because you're using a deodorant! A deodorant won't keep your skin clean.

Tattoos and Piercings

Any time your skin is broken, you risk introducing germs into your skin's lower layers, which may cause infections. That's one reason you need to think carefully before getting a tattoo or piercing, since both these procedures break the skin's surface.

Many teens like the idea of adding color and design to their skin. If you're thinking about getting a tattoo, it's a good idea to ask your local health department for recommendations. You want to be sure that the tattoo studio you choose is clean, safe, and professional. You might call or stop by first and ask the following questions:

- Do you use an autoclave? An autoclave is a device that sterilizes the needles and other tools using steam, pressure, and heat. The studio should allow you to watch as their equipment is sterilized in the autoclave.
- Is the tattoo artist a licensed practitioner? You may want to ask for references as well.
- Are "universal precautions" followed? The Occupational Safety and Health Administration (OSHA) has outlined these procedures that should be followed when dealing with blood and other body fluids.

If a tattoo salon doesn't answer yes to any of these questions, or if it looks dirty, find somewhere else to get your tattoo. Otherwise, you place yourself at risk of developing various skin infections like dermatitis and impetigo (see chapters 3 and 4). You also may contract even more serious diseases, such as HIV, hepatitis, and TUBERCULOSIS.

Once you have a tattoo, you need to take care of it until it is completely healed. Keep it covered and protect it with an antibi-

otic cream; if you think you might have contracted an infection, call your doctor right away. For the rest of your life, you'll need to wear sunscreen on the tattoo with at least SPF 30, since the dyed skin is more vulnerable to the sun's harmful rays.

A tattoo is intended to be a permanent part of your skin, so be certain you want to live with it for the rest of your life. (Tattoos can be removed, but the process is expensive and the results are sometimes unsatisfactory.) What you think is really cool at this point in your life may possibly seem like an embarrassment

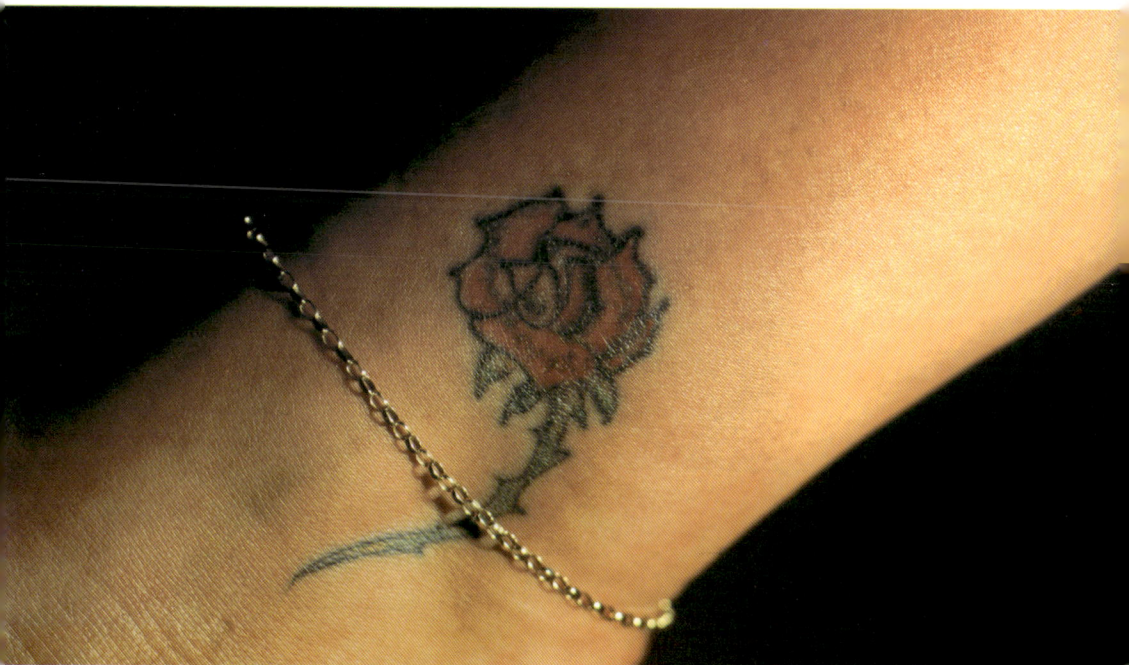

More Ways to Care For Your Skin

when you're at a different place further down the road. You also need to be aware that even with the safest, cleanest tattoo salons, there are some risks. If you already have a skin condition like eczema (see chapter 3), the tattoo process may cause you to have a flare-up. Some people have allergic reactions to the tattoo pigments, and other people develop the thick scars called keloids (see chapter 2). If you find a clean, professional tattoo studio, the risks are low—but you need to be certain getting a tattoo is worth those risks.

The same is true when it comes to body piercing. Make sure you get your piercing only in a shop that is clean and sterilizes everything in an autoclave. Avoid shops that use piercing

Healthy Skin

guns, as these aren't sterile; needles that are disposed after every use are safer. The piercer should also use disposable gloves and a mask that are changed between each customer. Don't pierce yourself or have a friend do it; the odds are good that your bedroom or your friend's kitchen is not the most sterile of places!

When you think about whether a piercing is right for you, keep in mind the following risks:

·   chronic infection
·   prolonged bleeding
·   scarring

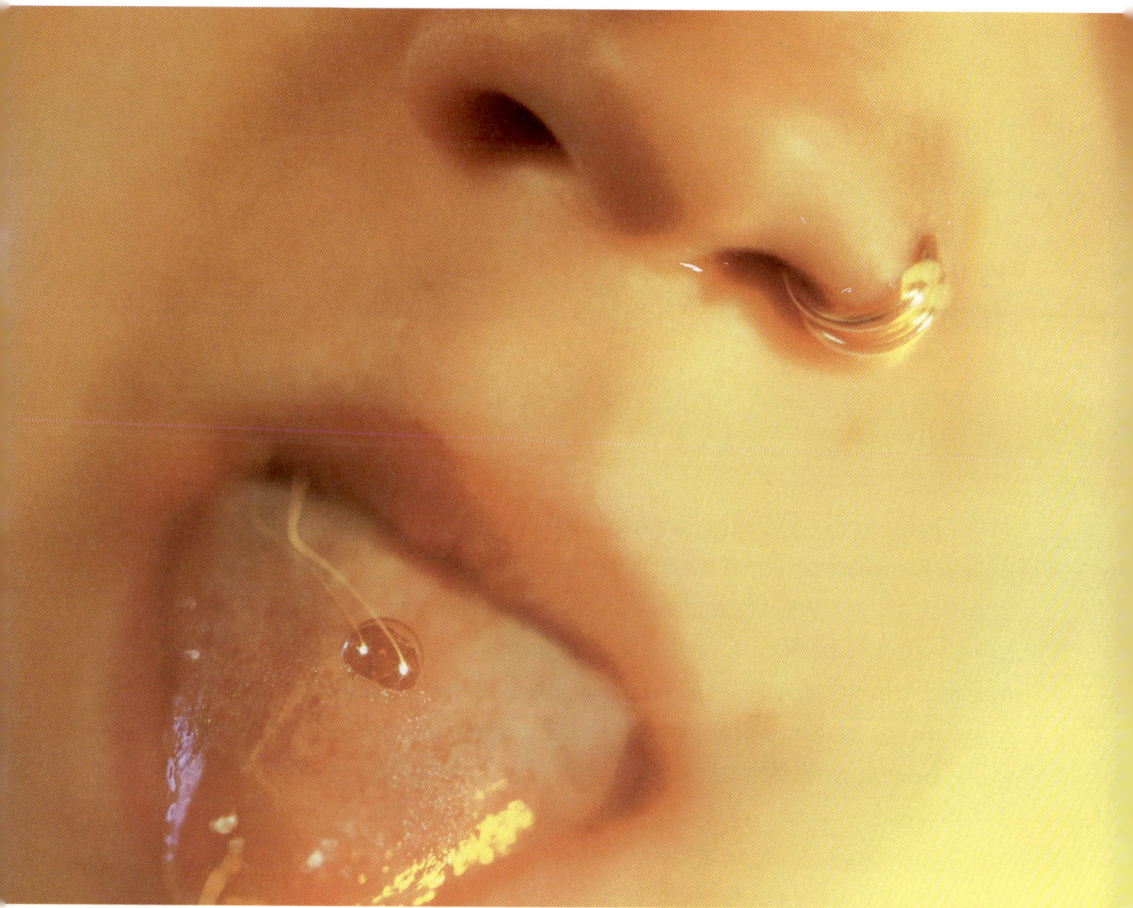

- hepatitis B and C (which can be fatal)
- tetanus
- HIV (although there are no documented cases of anyone catching HIV from a piercing)
- skin allergies to the jewelry
- abscesses or boils that form at the site of the piercing from staph infections (see chapter 4)
- chipped or broken teeth from mouth jewelry
- choking from mouth jewelry
- a speech impediment from mouth jewelry
- pain
- the destruction of the cartilage in your nose or ear
- tears in your skin that can lead to permanent large holes
- a loss of taste sensation from mouth jewelry

If you consider all the risks and decide that a piercing is still right for you, be sure to take good care of it. Don't touch it without washing your hands first. (Remember those staph germs we discussed in chapter 4?) Keep the area clean with soap (not alcohol, which can dry the skin and cause irritation). If you have

The American Dental Association opposes oral (tongue, lip, or cheek) piercing—and the American Academy of Dermatology is against all forms of body piercing except the ear lobe (and possibly the belly button). Both the U.S. and Canadian Red Cross won't accept blood donations from anyone who has had a piercing that may have been performed with unsterile tools within the past year, because the procedure can transmit dangerous blood-borne diseases.

Healthy Skin

a mouth piercing, protect the skin inside your mouth by using an antibacterial mouthwash after you eat.

Your skin is right out there where everyone can see. If you want to express yourself through piercing and tattooing your skin, then be sure to take the necessary safety precautions. And make sure this is a decision you can live with for the rest of your life!

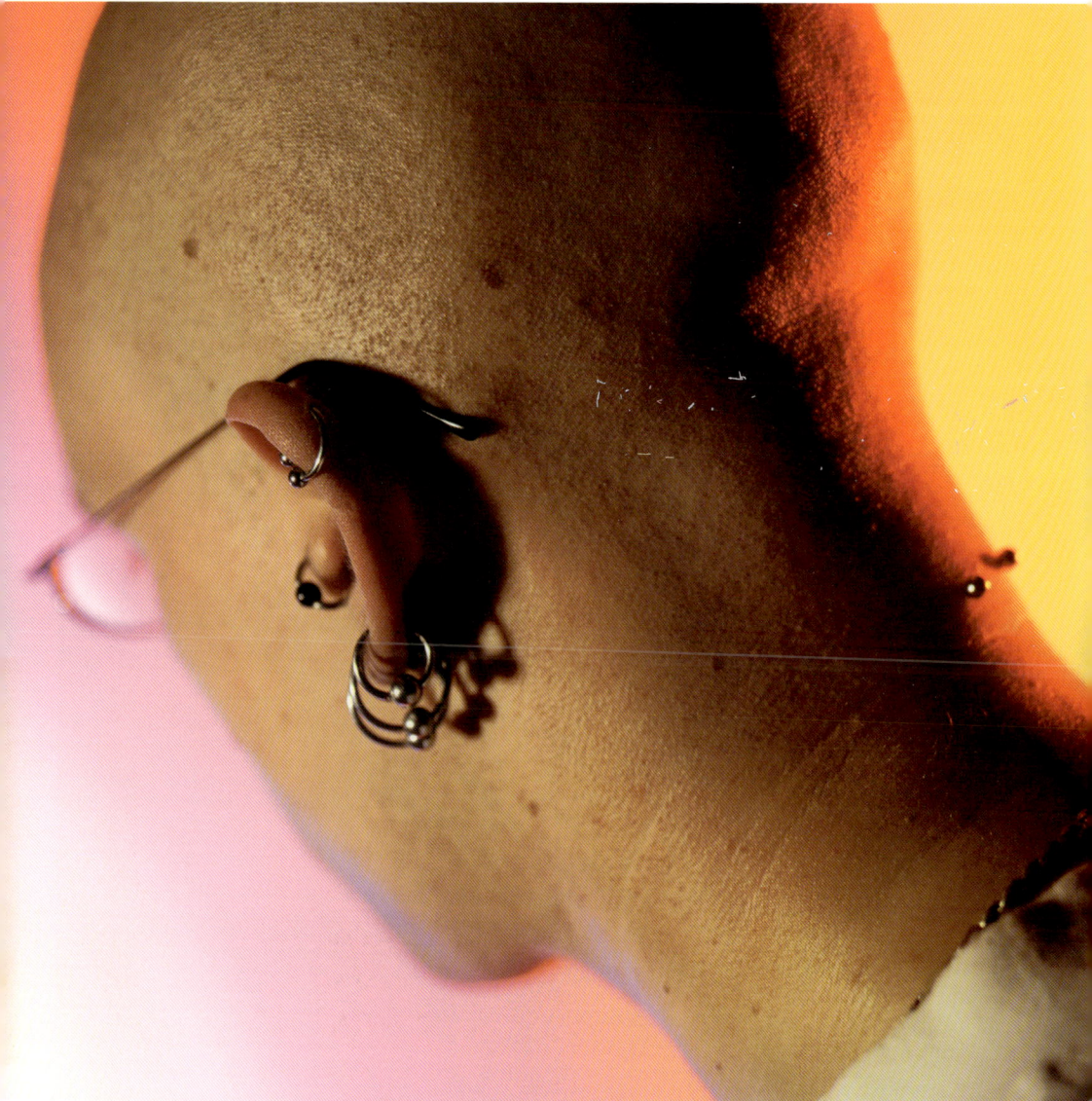

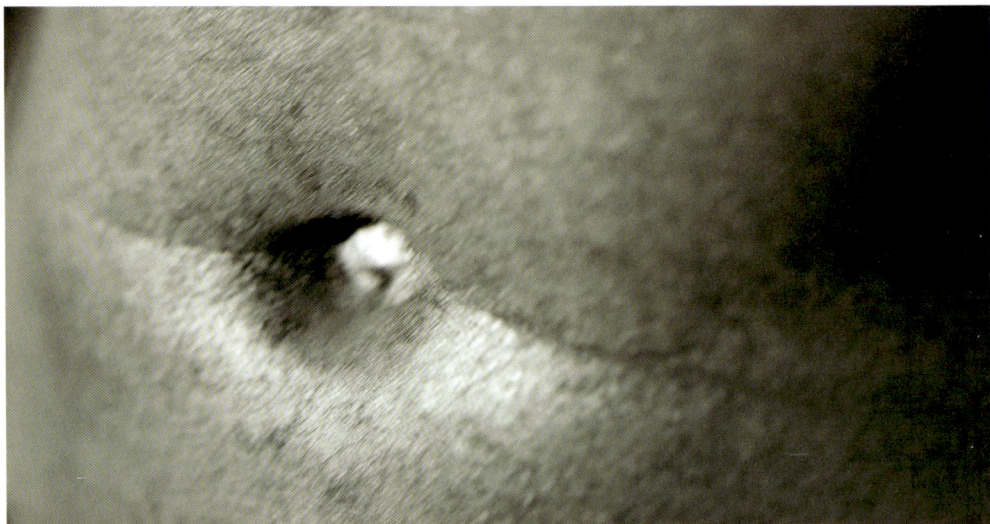

Unlike other body parts, your ear lobe and belly button are made of fatty tissue and have a good blood flow—which means they're less vulnerable to permanent damage and infection.

Healthy Skin

Diet

What you eat can affect your skin's health. The vitamins and nutrients in certain foods can contribute to the way your skin looks. Here is a list of "face-friendly" foods:

- Dark, leafy greens like spinach, turnip greens, and kale contain ANTIOXIDANTS and zinc. Zinc helps to break down damaged collagen (the stuff that keeps your skin from drooping), allowing new collagen to form, and it may also help to fight acne.
- Orange vegetables and fruits—carrots, squash, sweet potatoes, cantaloupe, apricots, peaches—are high in vitamin A, which boosts your resistance to infection (and will help your skin fight the germs that cause acne and other skin conditions).
- Citrus fruits (oranges, lemons, grapefruits) contain lots of vitamin C, which helps keep skin elastic and prevents bruising. Your skin also uses vitamin C to reconstruct collagen.
- Vitamin E—found in nuts—is also good for your skin.
- Fish (especially salmon, mackerel, trout, and bass) contain special oils called omega-three fatty acids. These oils battle the FREE RADICALS that can damage your skin's collagen. Ground flaxseed added to your breakfast cereal is another good way to get omega-three fatty acids.
- Soy foods (tofu and soy beans) contain a chemical that acts like ESTROGEN. This chemical may help prevent acne flare-ups by balancing women's hormones.
- Oatmeal's fiber helps filter TOXINS from your body, which will also help clear your skin. Oatmeal is also rich in the B vitamins that aid new skin-cell growth.

In a research study conducted in Sweden, acne-prone patients who were give zinc supplements found that 85 percent of their blemishes disappeared after three months.

A well-balanced diet will help you keep your skin clear and smooth. Some foods and drinks, however, can put your skin's health in jeopardy:

- The saturated fats found in red meat, ice cream, and butter encourage the growth of free radicals, which will contribute to your skin's aging.
- Caffeine is a DIURETIC; in other words, when you drink coffee or colas, you're actually sapping your body—and your skin—of moisture. If you do drink coffee or cola, down a glass of water afterward to counteract the effects of the caffeine.
- Abusing alcohol regularly can dilate the tiny blood vessels in your skin, giving your skin a red, flushed appearance. Alcohol, like caffeine, can also cause DEHYDRATION, so it's a good idea to drink one or two glasses of water for every alcoholic drink you consume.

The body you have now is the only one you'll ever get. You may not think very often about getting older, but the same body you have now is the one you'll have when you're thirty—and fifty—and seventy. If you want to keep your body well and strong for a long time, you'll need to take care of it—and

Healthy Skin

keeping your skin healthy by practicing good diet and hygiene habits is one good way to protect your body from infection, disease, and aging.

Further Reading

Callan, Annette. *All About Skin Care*. New York: Oxford, 2000.

Ceaser, Jennifer. *Everything You Need to Know About Acne*. New York: Rosen, 2000.

Dubrow, Terry J. and Brenda D. Adderly. *Acne Cure*. Emmaus, Penn.: Rodale, 2003.

Lees, Mark. *Skin Care: Beyond the Basics*. Clifton Park, N.Y.: Milady Publishing, 2001.

Leffell, David. *Total Skin: The Definitive Guide to Whole Skin Care for Life*. New York: Hyperion, 2000.

McNally, Robert Aquinas. *Skin Health Information for Teens: Health Tips About Dermatological Concerns and Skin Cancer Risks*. Detroit, Mich.: Omnigraphics, 2003.

Papadopoulos, Linda and Carl Walker. *Understanding Skin Problems*. New York: John Wiley and Sons, 2003.

For More Information

American Academy of Dermatology
www.aad.org

American Cancer Society
www.cancer.org

Melanoma … the ABC's
www.melanoma.com

National Cancer Institute Cancer Information Service
www.cancer.gov

National Council on Skin Care Prevention
www.skincancerprevention.org

National Eczema Association for Science and Education
www.nationaleczema.org

National Eczema Society
www.eczema.org

National Institute of Arthritis and Musculoskeletal and Skin Diseases (NIAMS)
www.niams.nih.gov

National Psoriasis Foundation
www.psoriasis.org

National Vitiligo Foundation
www.mynivfi.org

Skin Care
www.skincarephysicians.com

The Sun Safe Project
www.cancer.dartmouth.edu/melanoma/sunsafe.shtml

TeensHealth
www.kidshealth.org

What You Need to Know About Skin Cancer
www.cancer.gov/cancerinfo/wyntk/skin

Publisher's note:
The websites listed on these pages were active at the time of publication. The publisher is not responsible for websites that have changed their addresses or discontinued operation since the date of publication. The publisher will review and update the websites upon each reprint.

Glossary

ADRENAL INSUFFICIENCY   An autoimmune disorder caused by the adrenal gland not producing enough of the hormone called corticosteroid.

AIDS   A disease of the human immune system (acquired immunodeficiency syndrome) caused by infection with HIV.

ALOPECIA AREATA   An autoimmune disorder that causes patches of baldness.

ANTIBIOTICS   Substances that inhibit or kill microorganisms.

ANTIBODIES   The protective proteins produced by the body's immune system to fight germs (bacteria and viruses) or other foreign substances.

ANTIOXIDANTS   Substances that inhibit oxidation, a process that contributes to aging and vulnerability to disease.

AUTOIMMUNE DISEASES   Disorders in which a person's immune system reacts against the body's own organs or tissues.

BIOPSY   The removal and examination of tissue, cells, or fluids from the living body.

CHRONIC   Marked by long duration or frequent occurrence.

DANDER   Tiny scales from hair, feathers, or skin that may trigger allergic reactions.

DEHYDRATION   An abnormal loss of body fluids.

DEPIGMENTATION   Loss of pigment (the material that gives color to body cells) in the skin, hair, mucous membranes, or retina of the eye.

DERMATOLOGIST   A medical doctor whose specialty is the skin and its structure, functions, and diseases.

DIURETIC   A substance that increases the flow of urine.

EPIDEMIC   An outbreak or product of sudden rapid spread, growth, or development.

ESTROGEN   A substance (as a sex hormone) tending to promote estrus ("heat") and stimulate the development of female secondary sex characteristics.

FILAMENTS   Single threads or thin flexible threadlike objects.

FOOD AND DRUG ADMINISTRATION   The FDA is a U.S. federal agency authorized by Congress to inspect, test, approve, and set safety standards for foods and food additives, drugs, cosmetics, and medical devices.

FREE RADICALS   Especially reactive atoms or groups of atoms that may combine with chemicals within the body, allowing them to do harm.

GENES   The packages of hereditary information on a chromosome.

GRANULOSE   Having a grainy texture.

HEPATITIS   Inflammation of the liver.

HIV   Human immunodeficiency viruses are any of a group of retroviruses that infect and destroy helper T cells of the immune system.

HORMONES   Products of living cells that circulate in body fluids or sap and produce a specific effect on the activity of cells remote from their point of origin.

HYPERTHYROIDISM   An autoimmune disease caused by an overly active thyroid gland.

HYPOTHALAMUS   The region of the brain that contains a control center for many functions of the autonomic nervous system, and has important links with the endocrine system because of its complex interaction with the pituitary gland.

IMMUNE SYSTEM   The bodily system that protects the body from foreign substances, cells, and tissues by producing the immune response.

LESIONS   Abnormal changes in structure of an organ or part due to injury or disease.

LOCAL ANESTHETIC An agent which produces a loss of sensation in one specific area.

LYMPH GLANDS The organs that filter the flow of lymph.

METASTASIZE Transfer of a disease-producing agency from the site of disease to another part of the body.

NUCLEUS The "brain" of a cell that contains DNA and controls the cell's activity.

ORAL CONTRACEPTIVES "The Pill," taken by mouth, which uses the hormones estrogen and progesterone to prevent pregnancy by interfering with ovulation.

OXIDIZES Breaks down by combining with oxygen.

PATHOLOGIST A medical specialist who interprets and diagnoses the changes caused by disease in tissues and body fluids.

PERNICIOUS ANEMIA An autoimmune disease where the body fails to absorb vitamin B12, causing a low level of red blood cells.

PIGMENT A substance that imparts color to other materials.

PUBERTY The period (usually the early teenage years) of becoming first capable of reproducing, sexually marked by the maturing of the genital organs, and the development of secondary sex characteristics.

PUBIC Of, relating to, or situated in or near the region of the three principal bones composing either half of the pelvis (the crotch area).

RESISTANT Capable of resisting or opposing infection or other injury.

SCABIES A contagious itch that is caused by parasitic mites.

SIDE EFFECTS Secondary and usually adverse effects (as of a drug).

STEROIDS Any of numerous compounds containing a 17-carbon 4-ring system and including the sterols and various hormones and glycosides; often used as a medication, although it often produces side effects.

SUTURES Strands or fibers used to sew parts of the living body.

SYNTHETIC Artificial or manmade; something that does not occur naturally.

THYROID An endocrine gland situated in the throat below the voice box that secretes hormones vital to metabolism and growth.

TOPICAL Designed for application and action on the the skin.

TOXINS Poisonous substances.

TUBERCULOSIS A highly variable communicable disease of humans and some other vertebrates characterized by toxic symptoms or allergic manifestations that in humans primarily affect the lungs.

ULTRAVIOLET Situated beyond the visible spectrum at its violet end, having a wavelength shorter than wavelengths of visible light and longer than those of X rays.

Index

Picture Credits

Artville pp. 20, 38 44, 52, 55, 62, 71, 80, 86, 89, 93, 97, 101, 102
Corel p. 83
Eye Wire pp. 28, 107
iDream p. 10
Gurinaleksandr | Dreamstime.com: p. 98
Image Source pp 35
Autumn Libal pp. 19, 26
Life Art pp. 25, 31, 47, 48, 64, 76, 77
PhotoAlto pp. 59, 114, 114
PhotoDisc pp. 22, 50, 104, 110
Ellyn Sanna pp. 13, 14, 17, 18
Ben Stewart pp. 56, 75, 77, 87, 91
Stockbyte pp. 109, 111, 113, 117
Studio One p. 94

The individuals in these images are models, and the images are for illustrative purposes only.

To the best knowledge of the publisher, all other images are in the public domain. If any image has been inadvertantly un-credited or miscredited, please notify Vestal Creative Services, Vestal, New York 13850, so that rectification can be made for future printings.

Biographies

Rae Simons has written many novels and young adult nonfiction. She lives in New York State.

Mary Ann McDonnell, Ph.D., R.N., is the owner of South Shore Psychiatric Services, where she provides psychiatric services to children and adolescents. She has worked as a psychiatric nurse at Franciscan Hospital for Children and has been a clinical instructor for Northeastern University and Boston College advanced-practice nursing students. She was also the director of clinical trials in the pediatric psychopharmacology research unit at Massachusetts General Hospital. Her areas of expertise are bipolar disorder in children and adolescents, ADHD, and depression.

Dr. Sara Forman is a board certified physician in Adolescent Medicine. She has worked at Bentley Student Health Services since 1995 as a Senior Consulting Physician. Dr. Forman graduated from Barnard College and Harvard Medical School and completed her residency in Pediatrics at Children's Hospital of Philadelphia. After completing a fellowship in Adolescent Medicine at Children's Hospital Boston (CHB), she became an attending physician in that division. Dr. Forman's specialties include general adolescent health and eating disorders. She is the Director of the Outpatient Eating Disorders Program at Children's Hospital in Boston. In addition to seeing students at Bentley College, Dr. Forman sees primary care adolescent patients in the Adolescent Clinic at Children's and at The Germaine Lawrence School, a residential school for emotionally disturbed teenage girls.

CANE RIDGE